SUCCESS THROUGH STILLNESS

SUCCESS THROUGH STILLNESS

MEDITATION MADE SIMPLE

RUSSELL SIMMONS

WITH CHRIS MORROW

GOTHAM
BOOKS

GOTHAM BOOKS
Published by the Penguin Group
Penguin Group (USA) LLC
375 Hudson Street
New York, New York 10014

USA | Canada | UK | Ireland | Australia | New Zealand | India | South Africa | China
penguin.com
A Penguin Random House Company

LIBRARY OF CONGRESS CATALOGING-IN-PUBLICATION DATA
Simmons, Russell.
   Success through stillness : meditation made simple / Russell Simmons, with Chris Morrow.
     pages cm
   ISBN 978-1-592-40865-8 (hardback)
  1. Meditation—Therapeutic use.   2. Self-care, Health.   3. Mind and body.
I. Morrow, Chris.   II. Title.
   RC489.M43S555 2014
   615.8'528—dc23   2013043493

Printed in the United States of America
10 9 8 7 6 5 4 3 2 1
5327   5284   3/14
Set in Adobe Garamond Pro
Designed by Elke Sigal

Dedicated to my two daughters,
Ming Lee and Aoki Lee.

With a special dedication
to their mother, Kimora Lee,
for naming my last two books
when I wasn't sure what to call them.

CONTENTS

CONTENTS

SUCCESS THROUGH STILLNESS

PART ONE

Why Meditate?

CHAPTER 1

THE PATH TO HAPPINESS

*Life finds its purpose and fulfillment
in the expansion of happiness.*

MAHARISHI MAHESH YOGI

Why should you meditate?

The answer is very simple: to be happy.

Which is the only reason you're here.

That might sound like a very simple take on the meaning of life, but I believe it with every fiber in my body.

Yes, I'm certain that if we were to strip away our egos, desires, fears, and insecurities, all that would be left is happiness.

There are days where it feels like we can almost touch this truth. Days where when we wake up, the sun seems to be shining a little brighter, the birds are singing a little bit louder, and we walk out into the world with a bounce in our step and a song in our heart.

Yet there are also days when we start out feeling nervous about what lies ahead of us, unsure about the situations we're about to encounter. Where it could be eighty degrees and sunny out, but we feel like we're walking through a cold, dark world.

The purpose of this book is to show you that you can control which of those worlds you live in. You can decide that no matter what is happening around you, the sun will always be shining in your world.

Or you can decide that your world is always going to be a cold, dark place.

The point is, the external world doesn't make that choice.

You do.

Obviously most people would prefer to live in the sunshine. The problem is that they just don't know how to step into it.

I'm here to tell you that meditation can take you there. That sitting in silence for twenty minutes can be a tool to wash away the pain, frustration, and insecurities that have been coloring your existence and allow you to get back to the state of happiness that is your birthright.

The path that I will lay out in this book represents the simplest route between your current state and that happiness. As your guide, I will not lead you on any detours or suggest that we take the more scenic route. No, this is a simple and straightforward guide on how to use the tool of meditation to get the most out of your life— written with the authority of someone who has used that very tool every day for the past fifteen years himself.

I want to keep this book very simple and direct in order to help demystify meditation. To clear up any misconceptions or uneasiness that you might have about this ancient practice and help you see that it's a valuable and relevant tool in the modern world. Just the fact that you're reading these words means that at the very least you're curious about the practice, but maybe there's still something that's holding you back from committing fully. Maybe you still have a vague sense that there's something "foreign" or "mystical" about meditation. Even worse, something "ungodly." Or maybe you're still skeptical that it "really" works. Or maybe—and this one always makes me laugh—you believe that it could help you, but you're just too "busy" to meditate.

I'll dive into these misconceptions, and several other ones, over the course of the book, but let me say right here that there is nothing "foreign" about meditation. In fact, it's way more mainstream than you probably realize. Oprah. Jerry Seinfeld. Paul McCartney. Phil Jackson. Ellen DeGeneres. Forest Whitaker. These are all people that you know of and whose success has inspired millions of people. And they all meditate and credit the practice as one of the foundations of their success. I'll be sharing their thoughts on meditation, and the thoughts of many leaders from the arts, business, education, science, and the spiritual communities, throughout the book, because I want you to realize that when you become a meditator, you are joining a community of successful people. A community of people who move through life on their own terms and maximize their potential.

To share an example that really illustrates this point, earlier this year I bumped into Dwyane Wade and Chris Bosh of the NBA's Miami Heat at a party Dwyane and Gabrielle Union were hosting in Malibu. It was not long after the Heat had just won their second straight championship, and after I congratulated Dwyane and Chris, we got to talking about practices they could use to stay energized and focused. I told them how much meditation had helped me maintain focus in my career and suggested they give it a try.

"You guys should definitely try it, because though you might not realize it, you've already experienced the sort of focus and stillness meditation creates," I told them. "You know how when you get out on the court and get in a zone? When it feels like the basket is as big as an ocean and every time you put up a shot, you just know it's going to go in? Well, meditation is going to help you get in that zone *off* the court too. Imagine being able to *live* in that sort of focus."

They were both incredibly intrigued. "Everything we do is about trying to find more precision, more focus when we're out on the court," Dwayne said. "To figure out how to push ourselves into that zone. Do you really think meditation could help do that?"

"I'll put it to you like this," I said. "The Chinese philosopher Lao Tzu once said, 'To the mind that is still, the whole universe surrenders.' Well, meditation stills your mind. Completely. So if the whole universe is going to surrender to a still mind, imagine what an opposing team will do. They're just going to lay right down!"

They both laughed, but they also both made a point of asking me for advice on how to get started. So I put them in touch with Bob

Roth, a great friend and meditation teacher of mine who's been teaching the practice for more than forty years—in fact, he's the person who taught some of the folks I just mentioned, including Oprah and Ellen. But I'm definitely going to send them a copy of this book too in case they never followed up with Bob.

It was conversations like that, and many, many others that I've had over the years, that inspired me to write this book. Because while it's great if Dwyane Wade can use meditation to become an even greater player, the best thing I could do with the knowledge I've acquired over the years is share Lao Tzu's message with everyone and anyone who'll listen: To the mind that is still, the whole universe will surrender.

And meditation is both the easiest and most effective tool at your disposal to calm down your turbulent mind.

I realize a lot of you have probably come to these pages because you're looking to duplicate the kind of success I've enjoyed in my field, that Dwyane Wade has had in his or Oprah in hers. So let me say without any reservation that I consider meditation to be the most effective tool that you can employ to build a similar success in your own life.

But aside from the ways meditation will help you improve your career, I'm also going to speak on the many other benefits it will bring to your day-to-day life: decreased stress, improved health (especially your nervous system), better eating habits, and increased focus.

And those are just some of the more tangible benefits. I'm also going to talk about how meditation will bring a sense of peace, compassion, and balance into your life. Those might sound like vague or unnecessary concepts—you might be thinking, "Just teach me how to be more successful and healthier and I'll be good"—but if I weren't promoting them, then I'd really just be wasting your time.

Sure, you could use meditation to help you make more money, or get ahead in your field, or even become healthier, but without a sense of peace and compassion in your life, you'll really be no better off than when you first picked up this book.

This idea of looking past material success and finding sustainable, long-term happiness inside yourself was also at the heart of my most recent book, *Super Rich: A Guide to Having It All*. I'd encourage you to check it out if anything in these pages resonates with you. In fact, one of the reasons I decided to put this book together is because so many people came up to me after *Super Rich* was published and told me that the chapter on meditation had changed their lives. That for the first time, instead of reacting to their thoughts and emotions, they were actually in control of them. Instead of feeling aimless and unsure about the direction their lives were headed in, through meditation they felt confident and empowered.

I know the feeling. Since I first embraced the practice over fifteen years ago, I've meditated every day. No matter where I am or what's on my schedule, I won't walk out into the world until I've had twenty minutes of meditation. I've tried starting my day with coffee, with food, and even with drugs, but nothing comes close to getting me in the right frame of mind like meditation.

Which is why after I'm done singing the praises of the practice of meditation, I'm going to teach you how to *do it*.

In the most direct and accessible way possible, I'm going to show you how committing to twenty minutes of silence, twice a day, will radically transform how you feel about yourself and your relationship with the world.

But please don't jump ahead to that part yet. Even if you feel like you're already sold on the practice and just want to get right to it. This is a short book and I've tried not to put anything extra in here that's going to needlessly get in the way of your embracing this beautiful and simple practice. But it is important for you to learn about the effects meditation will have on you. Because as eager as you might be to start right now, I won't lie to you, committing to meditation will be a challenge. Twenty minutes twice a day might not sound like much right now, but when you also have to walk your dog in the morning, or make your kids' lunch and get them ready for school, or get yourself ready for work, or are even feeling hungover from the night before, suddenly it can be hard to find those minutes in the morning. Just as when you have to pick up your kids from basketball practice, answer a bunch of e-mails, pay a bunch of bills, make dinner, or finish an assignment for your class, it can be challenging to fit in those twenty minutes in the evening as well.

Which is why I really want you to familiarize yourself with as much of the benefits of meditation as possible. So that no matter how distracted you might get by the world and what's happening around you, you're still going to be motivated to get those twenty minutes in. And no matter how hectic your life might be feeling or how many pressing things you've still got on your to-do list, you'll understand that the best thing you can be doing at that time is to simply be still.

CHAPTER 2

THE MAKING OF A MEDITATOR

Long before the world starting calling me a "music mogul" or "the godfather of hip-hop," growing up in Hollis, Queens, my friends and family used to call me "Rush." As nicknames go it was a good one, because back then it seemed like nothing could hold my attention for more than a few minutes at a time.

Definitely not school. Or church on Sunday. Or a job. A pretty girl might hold it for a minute, but soon I'd be rushing after the next girl who passed me in the school hallways or on the streets.

Everything I did—the way I walked, talked, ate, and even slept—was rushed.

If I was growing up in Hollis today, there's no doubt I'd be diagnosed with a severe case of attention deficit/hyperactivity disorder and put on a *double* dose of Ritalin or Adderall. Thankfully, back then I was viewed as only being a bit "rambunctious."

I did come close to getting in some serious trouble coming up on the streets of Queens in the seventies. Put it this way: Melle Mel could have been talking about me and my friends in the early hip-hop hit "The Message" when he rapped about the "number book takers / Thugs, pimps and pushers and the big money makers" and how we wanted to "grow up to be just like them."

But despite doing some heavy flirting with that lifestyle, I could never go all the way with it. Even if I did have moments of admiration for those thugs and pushers, I also had an innate sense that there was something better for me out there too. And as I became a teenager and saw so many of my friends beginning to fall into the traps of petty crime, gangs, and addiction, I began to think, "I need to take a different path."

For me, that path led to hip-hop. At the time it might have looked like a dead end to most people, but it gave me the perfect outlet to express all the energy I was feeling on the streets of New York, but in a way that was positive and empowering instead of hurtful and destructive.

I'm not going to sit here and run down my list of accomplishments from those days—I'll assume that if you picked up this book, then you already know a little something about Kurtis Blow, Run-DMC, LL Cool J, the Beastie Boys, Public Enemy, and Def Jam Recordings (and if for some reason you don't, then just type those names into YouTube and prepare to get lost in some incredible music!).

But suffice it to say, I did experience a good deal of worldly success working with those MCs and a lot of other incredibly talented artists as well. In the ensuing years, I was able to find success in fashion, film, financial services, and now mostly philanthropic and social initiatives.

I've loved being able to build a bridge between the incredible culture of hip-hop and mainstream America. It has been inspiring work and I felt, and continue to feel, blessed to be doing it.

The irony is, however, that for many years I was way off base about what was driving my accomplishments. Certainly as a young man, I figured that the "secret to my success" was doing a lot of drugs, going to a lot of parties, sleeping with a lot of women, and chasing money wherever it might take me. After all, that's the lifestyle I was living and people kept telling me how great I was doing, so there had to be a connection, right?

I couldn't see it at the time, but in retrospect nothing could have been farther from the truth. The inspiration that helped me become a champion for hip-hop didn't come from driving around in a limousine, it came from a quiet moment in the studio working on the final mix for Run-DMC's "Rock Box" and thinking, "I want to share this incredible feeling with the world."

Just as the inspiration that helped me create my clothing line Phat Farm didn't come from sniffing coke in a club surrounded by models, but rather from the sense of peace and tranquility I got when I looked at the sketches for a new jacket and felt myself getting lost in the beauty of the design. Those rare moments of stillness, not the chaotic life I had created, were the foundations of my happiness and success.

Today, there is zero doubt in my mind that if I had kept on believing that the noise was what was fueling me, my life would have fallen apart. When my records had stopped being "hot" or my clothes had stopped being "cool" (which is inevitable in those sorts of industries), I would have figured, "Hmmm. I really need another big record. Better find some more parties and go get high." But chasing more drugs or parties wouldn't have made me even a centimeter more successful. Or happy. Or creative. And obviously it could have made my life a lot worse if it got in the way of my work or took away my focus, or turned me into an addict or empty party boy.

What I thought was inspiration was really nothing but noise. And if I had kept stuffing that noise into my head, the less and less I would have been able to hear those quiet moments that I actually needed so badly. I would have kept pushing myself to what I thought was the top of the mountain, but in reality I would have just been setting myself up for a terrible fall.

Thankfully, I never had to experience that sort of fall. Despite the reckless lifestyle I was living, I never actually crashed and burned like so many of the other people I was racing around town with in those days. I didn't have to lose my job and my house, or go into rehab, to realize that I had been chasing the wrong things. Instead, I was able to slow down and see that my success had always been in those moments of stillness that I'd experienced. And that the more I could access that stillness, then the more happiness and success I could experience.

I can honestly say that without that stillness, there's no way I'd be where I am today. Not only professionally, but personally and spiritually too. After over thirty years in the entertainment industry, I still wake up as excited to go to work every day as I did the first day Rick Rubin and I opened Def Jam Recordings. I can honestly say that whatever I'm going to do tomorrow has me as excited and energized as I felt when Run-DMC was about to go onstage at Live Aid, when Public Enemy was about to release *It Takes a Nation of Millions to Hold Us Back*, or when I put Jay Z on the *Nutty Professor* soundtrack and watched the world fall in love with him. It's an incredible blessing to be able to feel as energized and focused in my fifties as I did in my twenties and thirties.

But even more important, I also wake up every day knowing that I'm in a great place with the people closest to me—my beautiful daughters, Ming Lee and Aoki; their mother, Kimora Lee; and my brothers, Danny and Joey. It's a tremendous comfort to know that no matter what little disagreements, frustrations, or setbacks I might have during the course of a day, at the end of it nothing is going to change the love I share with my family. It certainly provides me with more comfort than any gold plaque on my wall or fancy car in my garage ever did. Every day, I'm so thankful that I know what it means to operate out of stillness.

I won't lie, it did take me a long time to get here. Years and years in fact. As I'm quick to tell people, I had to do a lot of damage before I finally accepted that I liked early-morning meditation better than late-night drinking. But once I did come to that realization, there was no turning back.

THE YOGA CONNECTION

For me, the first step in leaving the partying lifestyle behind came when I walked into a yoga studio. As I've shared many times before, my initial motivation for going to a yoga class wasn't to help me get centered spiritually or even to get my limbs more limber—it was because I thought it would be a great place to meet beautiful women. And man, was it ever!

But while beautiful women might have been what lured me in, it was something else entirely that kept me coming back. Sitting on my yoga mat and simply focusing on my breath, my crazy, hectic, and often out-of-control life began to slow down. All the anxieties and stresses that had consumed my day up until that point suddenly didn't feel so urgent, so pressing anymore.

I could almost feel all the noise rushing out of my head, like someone had untied a balloon. To be able to see my thoughts slowly come in and go out of my mind, instead of having them rush through my mind like a runaway train, was the greatest feeling.

I can call it great now, but truth be told, that sense of stillness was very scary at first. I was "Rush," after all. The guy who talked a mile a minute and always had a cell phone glued to his ear (before everyone else looked that way too!). The guy who was constantly on a mission to make more money, have sex with more women, and snort more coke than the next man. And who had experienced a lot of "success" living that way.

That's how I saw myself. I didn't know who this peaceful, calm, and centered guy sitting on the mat with a silly grin on his face was. A guy who couldn't have cared less about parties, money, or material success (I'll admit I'm still working on the women part). Suddenly my identity felt like it was at stake. And even worse at the time, my money. I remember walking out of that first yoga class, turning to my friend Bobby Shriver, and saying, "If I keep doing this shit, I'm going to lose all my money!"

Bobby and I still laugh about that moment today, because as I've said, nothing could have been farther from the truth. Far from making me lose my "golden touch," that sense of stillness I experienced in yoga, and later in meditation, actually was what prolonged and saved my career.

After getting past that initial moment of doubt, I became incredibly focused on experiencing that sense of stillness again and again. The stillness that reminded me that I could be a better person, a better friend, a better citizen of the world, as well as a better businessman.

Soon I found myself going to yoga every single day if I could fit it into my schedule. (Nowadays, fitting yoga into my schedule isn't even a question. My assistants automatically know to set aside time for a yoga class no matter where I am in the world. And people who really know me always ask to have their meetings with me scheduled for after my class because they know I'll be much more calm and focused.)

The stillness I experienced in yoga was such a welcome relief from the chaos of my life at that time. What was even greater was the "high" I'd feel once class was over, when both my body and mind felt completely tuned in and energized. If there was a problem, it was only that sometimes I couldn't quite hold on to that high as long as I wanted to.

I'd get out of class feeling incredibly peaceful and calm, only to find out that I had an "important" message waiting for me that I needed to respond to at once. Five minutes later I'd be arguing over record royalties or the release date of a new clothing line, and that stillness would be lost to the distractions of the world.

Or it might not have been anything as dramatic as a business dispute. Many times I remember walking out of class feeling completely at ease, when suddenly there would be a loud noise like a car honking or a door slamming. And then poof! The stillness was gone and instantly I'd be back to my distracted self.

So like a lot of people who really cherish that hour on the yoga mat, I started to look for ways that I could stretch the stillness. How I could take those moments of clarity I was experiencing during yoga class and extend them into the rest of my day.

It was that quest that led me to the practice of meditation. I don't remember one person in particular pulling me aside and telling me that I needed to meditate, or having an "aha" moment when I realized that meditation was going to change my life. Instead, I began to realize that many of the people whom I practiced yoga with also practiced meditation and seemed equally committed to both practices. Eventually I figured I'd try it myself.

I didn't know it at the time, but the progression from yoga to meditation is a very natural one, because at their essence they're really the same thing. To some, that might be hard to see; after all, how could something as physically challenging as yoga, which asks you to twist yourself up into a pretzel and stand on your head, have anything to do with meditation, which "just" asks you to sit in silence?

Yoga and meditation, however, are actually both part of what is known as the "eight limbs" of classical yoga. Despite having different outward appearances, both *dhyana* (meditation) and *asana* (the physical poses of yoga) are designed to take you to the same place, which is the stillness within your heart.

I know this isn't a book about yoga, but I really wanted to make that point. Because while I'm beyond excited that yoga has become such a large part of our cultural fabric over the past twenty years, I sense that not everyone understands what the goal of the yoga practice truly is.

It's not to lose weight or to get more toned (though you probably will). Or, as I have to keep reminding myself, to be around a lot of good-looking people (though you probably will too). The only goal of yoga is to help you become at peace.

The great Christian yogi Yogananda wrote that the actual term

THE EIGHT LIMBS OF YOGA

Yama: Universal morality

Niyama: Personal observances such as cleanliness, contentment, hard work, dedication, faith, and focus, as well as study of scripture

Asana (or Seat): Body poses and the physical practice of yoga

Pranayama: Breathing exercises and the control of life force

Pratyahara: Control of the senses

Dharana: Concentration on one's purpose in life

Dhyana: Meditation and devotion to the Divine

Samadhi: Union with the Divine

yoga should be defined as "cessation of the fluctuations of the mind caused by the afflictions." In other words, yoga isn't about getting our bodies in shape, it's about helping us calm our minds.

It's the same goal with meditation. Yet instead of standing on your head to achieve that peace, you simply sit down in a chair and close your eyes. Sounds a little bit more approachable, no?

But if meditation is such a simple way to achieve peace and happiness, then why do so many people seem reluctant to embrace the practice? Everywhere I look I see more and more new people coming to yoga. I think that's nothing short of a blessing for humanity, but I wish I saw the same number of people flocking to meditation.

I think part of it is that as humans we're drawn to group activities. As much as we like to complain about each other sometimes, we love being around other people. We get confidence and courage from seeing other people do something we'd like to try but aren't quite sure how to.

So if every day you see happy people with a smile on their face and a yoga mat on their back walk into a building, it's only a matter of time before you'll want to go in there and check out what's happening too. Or if every time you pick up a magazine or go to a website you see a picture of Gwyneth Paltrow or Jennifer Aniston headed to yoga class, eventually you might head to one too.

Meditation, on the other hand, doesn't have an easy-to-apply public face. While there are many group forms of meditation, from the outlawed Chinese Falun Gong to Quakers meeting for worship, the type of meditation I'm promoting in this book is usually practiced in solitude.

So while you might see pictures of me with my yoga mat and think, "Hmmm, Russell seems happy, maybe I should try that too," when you see a picture of Ellen DeGeneres or Oprah smiling, you might not make the connection that a large part of their peace comes from meditation.

Meditation's solitary nature is one reason it hasn't reached as many people—which is everyone—as it needs to. Another reason, which I'd like to address now, is that despite how accessible, easy, and inexpensive (can you get any cheaper than free?) the practice of meditation is, too many people still perceive that there are barriers between them and those twenty minutes of stillness.

So let's address some of them right now.

PART TWO

Why You *Think* You Can't Meditate

CHAPTER 3

I DON'T HAVE TIME

But, Russell, I just don't have time to meditate."

I can't tell you how many times I've heard this. I'm always getting approached by people looking for advice on how to "get ahead," but when I simply say, "Start meditating," they act like I just tried to duck the question! "Come on, Russell, I don't have time for all of that," they'll say in protest. "Give me something real!"

But I couldn't be more real with someone looking to improve their life than to tell them to meditate. So when they claim they don't have time, I always come back at them with that old saying about meditation: If you don't have *twenty minutes* to delve into yourself through meditation, then that means you really need *two hours*.

So if you're one of those people who claim that they would start meditating if they just had the time, my message to you is: Make the time.

That's because while your mind is the part of your body you use the most, it's also probably the part you spend the least amount of time taking care of.

Think about all the other parts of your life that you put real and sustained effort into maintaining.

If you are like millions and millions of us, you put *a lot* of effort into keeping your body in shape. That's obvious.

But we also put a lot of effort into maintaining our material possessions too. We take our shirts to the dry cleaner's when they're dirty and shine our shoes when they're scuffed. We polish our jewelry, wash our cars obsessively, and try to keep our lawns freshly mowed.

But how many hours do we spend trying to maintain our minds? In most cases, only the tiniest fraction in comparison. And in too many, virtually none at all!

In fact, pull out a piece of paper and make a checklist right now. Go down this list and write down how many hours a week you dedicate to maintaining these "essential" parts of your life:

- Your appearance (working out, brushing teeth, combing hair, shaving, putting on makeup, etc.)
- Your money (paying bills, following investments, planning for the future, etc.)
- Your clothes (shopping, washing, folding, ironing, etc.)

In addition to being one of the most talented entertainers of our generation, a father and a husband, Hugh Jackman is also a meditator. So what does he have to say to those who claim they don't have time for meditation? "Everyone takes a shower every day, and we don't complain about it. We do it out of discipline. There will always be an excuse not to meditate. . . . The ego says, 'You don't need to meditate, man. You're really busy. What about the kids?' But do I say, 'I can't shower today because I have to make time for the kids'?"

· Your home (cleaning, organizing, fixing, etc.)
· Your toys (fixing your car, playing video games, tinkering with the fixtures in your kitchen, etc.)

Add them up. Probably comes out to twenty to thirty hours a week, right?

Now add up how much time you spend maintaining your mind.

And remember, I'm not talking about *using* your mind. I'm talking about time that you dedicate *specifically* to relaxing and strengthening your mind.

Not much, huh?

Now let me ask you, have you ever felt, despite all the time you spend working out, cleaning up your house, balancing your checkbook, and organizing your paperwork, that your life is still always on the verge of falling apart? For all the effort you put into keeping things together, you're only a few inches from spiraling out of control?

If the answer is yes, then you need to make the time to meditate every day.

You're already working hard at having a productive, organized, and rewarding life. All I'm suggesting is you take some of that effort and direct it toward the place where you're really going to see an amazing return on your investment: your mind.

Let's look at the type of investment I'm asking for. Meditating twice a day for twenty minutes equals about four and a half hours a week. That's about an eighth of what you're spending on all those other aspects of your life.

I'm not saying stop brushing your teeth or paying your bills. But I know that when you don't get to the gym for a few days and start to feel sluggish and a little soft around the middle, you probably make it a priority to get to the gym the next morning. Or if you let the dishes pile up in your sink for a few days, you tell yourself, "I have to clean this up tomorrow morning. This is disgusting."

Well, you have to make meditation a similar priority in your life. That doesn't mean giving up going to the gym or going for a run or even watching TV in order to meditate. It just means that the same way you know you're not going to be happy if you don't make the time to work out or clean up your sink, you have to make the time to fit those forty minutes into your routine too.

But here's the thing: Once you start making that commitment, your crazy, hectic schedule isn't going to feel quite as hectic anymore. You're going to start feeling more balanced and less stressed out. The little things in life that always seemed to get you bent out of shape will become minor annoyances that you'll just shrug off. Instead of feeling like life is flying by you in a blur, you'll find yourself slowing down and being able to appreciate and enjoy all the beautiful things around you. To stop and smell the proverbial flowers.

I promise you that after a few months of consistent practice, instead of thinking, "Man, how am I going to find time to meditate today?" it's going to be a *given* that you're going to meditate. You might wonder how you'll find time to fit some other activities into your day, but meditating is always going to be at the top of your priority list.

I want you to consider this quote about finding the time to meditate from Ray Dalio, who runs Bridgewater Associates, one of the biggest investment funds in the world. Ray is an incredible innovator—he's been called the Steve Jobs of investing—and is personally responsible for billions of dollars in investment funds and hundreds of employees. If this guy isn't busy, then no one is.

Yet every day, twice a day, Ray sits down and meditates for twenty minutes. So when an interviewer from Georgetown University's Center for Meditation and Inter-religious Dialogue asked him what he had to say to people who claimed they were too busy to meditate, this was his reply:

It's twenty minutes in the morning, it's twenty minutes in the evening. And that's a challenging thing. It's the biggest reason that people leave it. But people who actually invest in it, experience it, and do it for more than six months, never stop doing it. And the reasons are, not only does it feel terrific at the time, but they carry it with them through the day. And it's really such an unbelievable investment. So when you're thinking about the twenty minutes you're putting in in the morning and the evening, and then you say how much does that change the effectiveness of my whole day, and the enjoyment of my whole day, it's such a radical payback, that you want to do it.

Ray really nailed it with that quote. Yes, finding twenty minutes twice a day is going to be a challenge at first. But once you face that challenge and start the practice, meditation is going to transition from something you feel like you have to do to something you want to do.

You just have to get started. And in this book I'm going to show you how.

CHAPTER 4

I'M NO GOOD AT IT

nother misconception that trips some people up is the belief that they're not "good" at meditating. These people make the effort to sit down and meditate but then don't stick with the practice because they feel like they're "doing it wrong" or somehow aren't having the same experience that "real" meditators do.

Maybe you're one of those people. Maybe you've tried to meditate before, but after a few minutes of sitting in silence you felt like it wasn't "working" and then gave up. If you fit that description, I want you to understand that what you experienced was very natural. In fact, it was what many people experience when they first start meditating.

But instead of giving up on the practice, after reading this book I want you to go back and try it again. Because no matter who you are or how you felt the first few times you tried, you do have the

SUCCESS THROUGH STILLNESS

potential to be a "great" meditator. If meditation were basketball, every single one of us would have Michael Jordan's natural ability. It's not like some of us would be short and couldn't jump, while others would be six foot six and be able to fly through the air! We'd all be like Mike. It would just be a question of accessing that ability.

The truth is *everyone* is great at meditation because it's our natural state. Saying you're not good at meditating is like saying you're not good at breathing. Or a fish saying that it's not good at swimming. It's impossible.

For example, a few years ago I went on Ellen DeGeneres's TV show and we started talking about meditation. Ellen told me that she had always wanted to meditate but had tried it a few times and—here comes the phrase again—"wasn't very good at it." So I told Ellen to try Transcendental Meditation (a mantra-based technique that's very similar to the one I'm going to teach you later in the book). She went home and tried, and after a few sessions she felt much more comfortable in the practice. Now Ellen meditates every day and credits it with giving her the focus she needs to keep her hectic life balanced—Ellen doesn't only have a talk show, she also runs a record label, does stand-up, and writes a blog and books of her own. She's got a lot on her plate. But when she went on the *Today* show, she said she meditates every day. "Because it feels good," she explained. "Kinda like when you have to shut your computer down, just sometimes when it goes crazy, you just shut it down and when you turn it on, it's okay again. That's what meditation is for me."

I'm so happy that Ellen gave meditation a second chance and now is doing so much to spread the word about the benefits of the practice. Hearing Ellen talk about her initial experience, I think what messed her up, and what messes up a lot of people, was the belief that because she was still having thoughts after she sat down to meditate and closed her eyes, she was doing something wrong.

I'm going to talk about the technique of dealing with your thoughts in much greater detail later on in the book, but for now I do want to say this:

Meditation does not mean the absence of thoughts.

Meditation does not mean going into a trance.

Meditation does not mean forgetting who or where you are.

If you're worrying that you're not "doing it right" because none of those things happen when you meditate, then please stop worrying.

Because you *will* have thoughts when you meditate.

It's just that meditation allows you to have a different relationship with your thoughts than you usually have. Instead of being overwhelmed or controlled by your thoughts, you get to detach yourself from them. So that you can stop making frantic, emotional decisions about who you are and what you want to do with your life and start choosing how you want to live in a controlled, peaceful, and contented manner.

Trust me, every day when I sit down and meditate, I still have thoughts in my head. *Lots* of them. I still think about issues I'm having at my office, or drama I'm dealing with in my personal life, or even something that happened in a movie I watched the night before. It's just that instead of becoming entangled in those thoughts, the longer I sit there in silence and focus on my mantra, the less and less "noise" they seem to make in my mind. To the point where after I've been sitting for a few minutes, the thoughts might come into my mind, but then they leave just as quickly. Which is when you start to experience a sense of peace and connectedness that is usually absent from your life. The sense of "shutting down your computer" that Ellen spoke of. But when Ellen used the phrase "shutting down," she wasn't talking about turning off her mind. She was talking about turning off the noise of the world. It's a critical distinction.

The first time you sit down and meditate, all your thoughts aren't going to go rushing out of your mind like air from an untied balloon. And that's fine. In fact, it's beautiful.

Just be patient and have faith that as long as you stick with your mantra and commit to the process of meditation, eventually that peace will come into your life. Or, as the great Japanese master Katagiri Roshi once put it, "Don't expect enlightenment—just sit down!"

Also, please don't think that you are either "too young" or "too old" to meditate. I taught my daughters meditation when they were both around ten, and they took to it like fish to water. Even a few years later, I'm sometimes surprised by how deep they are able to get into it.

Conversely, I taught it to a close family friend of ours named Victor (who used to be married to Kimora's mother and is a grandfather figure to our girls) when he was in his seventies, and he took to it just as easily. Today Victor meditates twice a day, every day, and credits it as one of the reasons he's able to bounce around with more energy than many men half his age.

But I do want to stress that while like my daughters and Victor you will see some positive effects from your meditation fairly rapidly—especially relating to your health and sense of well-being—meditation's true impact can take years, even decades, to be felt.

I recently watched a video of a speech that the Dalai Lama gave at Stanford University in which he said that even after sixty years of meditating, he was still surprised at how the practice continued to change him. He said that he started meditating at fifteen years old but didn't become "serious" about it until he was in his late twenties and early thirties, and didn't truly begin to reach "deeper levels" of consciousness until he was in his fifties and sixties. When asked by someone in the crowd what he learned from meditating all those years, the Dalai Lama said, "There is one thing I can state definitely, with confidence: The mind can change through training, through awareness. That's for sure."

I hope that what the Dalai Lama said really sinks in with you: The mind *can* change through training. So many people walk around saying, "My mind is too busy to meditate," or "I'm just not wired the right way for meditation." But the truth is, you are not trapped in a certain relationship with your emotions or your thoughts. No matter who you are or what you've gone through, you are capable of finding this peace.

You don't have to believe in your abilities as a meditator for it to work. You just have to take the time to do it.

That's it.

CHAPTER 5

I DON'T HAVE ANYWHERE
TO MEDITATE

This is another excuse that a lot of people fall back on when I encourage them to meditate. And to be fair, for a lot of people this is an issue. In a perfect world, everyone would have a quiet room in their home where they could get away from the noise and distractions, turn down the lights a little bit, and settle into those twenty minutes of silence. I won't lie, I have a room like that in my house and it's a great place to meditate.

But before you say, "Well, this isn't a perfect world and I don't have a room like that in my house, Russell," the point is that this world *is perfect*. It's just that until you slow down and access the stillness inside of you, sometimes it's hard to see that perfection.

So whether you have a mansion in Beverly Hills or live in a housing project in Harlem, remember that you *are* surrounded by perfect places to meditate. Some might seem better than others at first glance, but you can always find a good spot to sit in silence.

And even though I might have gone Hollywood in the last year or so, remember I spent most of my life in New York City, which is a noisy, busy place no matter how much money you've got or how many stories you live above the street. For example, my last apartment in New York City was directly across the street from the Ground Zero construction site, so even though I had a beautiful room with great light to meditate in, I still heard those bulldozers and cranes every time I sat down to meditate.

I'll talk more about how to deal with physical distractions while you meditate later on, but for now I just want to share a few tips on how to find a good place to meditate if you feel like you don't have one. Because after spending almost fifteen years meditating in NYC and sharing my experiences with other meditators, I've heard of people finding all sorts of inventive places to meditate.

One solution I've heard people come up with is meditating in a stairwell, which is a great option for people who might want to meditate at work. That might sound a little crazy to you at first, but stairwells don't get a lot of use during the day and as a result are usually pretty quiet. Unless the building you work in doesn't have an elevator, the biggest distraction you might encounter is a co-worker trying to sneak in a quick cigarette.

If there's enough room, I'd suggest bringing a folding chair into the hallway and sitting on that. If there isn't enough space, just keep an old pillow at your desk and sit on it on one of the landings. You might get a funny look from one of the smokers, but it will be more than worth it once you see how much more focused and rested you are every day at work.

Another good option is your car. While cars don't shut out every sound, they actually do cut down on a lot of noise. I have a friend who every day at work goes out to his car and spends the first twenty minutes of his lunch hour meditating. He even puts on a pair of sunglasses so that if his boss happens to walk by, he won't think he's trying to sleep off a hangover. He says that after a few minutes, whatever street noise he might hear begins to drift away, and he's usually able to get a very rewarding session in every day.

This also seems like a great solution for people who want to meditate at home but find that their kids, dogs, cats, or maybe even spouses don't seem capable of leaving them alone for twenty minutes. If that's your situation, head out to the driveway, sit down in your car, and catch your twenty minutes there. And if your kids or spouse still find a way to bother you out there, then just drive around the block and park. They'll learn that they can live without you for twenty minutes.

If leaving your house seems like too much of a hassle, then try meditating in your bathroom. When I included that tip in my book *Do You!*, I wasn't sure how people were going to take it. After all, the idea of sitting down on your toilet and repeating a mantra for twenty minutes might not be for everyone. But after the book came out, I was shocked how many people told me that they had tried it and found it to be very effective. I even had one guy tell me that he had been trying to meditate for years but could never find a spot where he felt comfortable. But after reading *Do You!*, he went into his bathroom, put a pillow on the toilet lid and another one behind his back, and had a very relaxing session. He's meditated every day since then—not always in his bathroom! But he told me that knowing he could always find a place in his apartment to meditate was the breakthrough that he needed to finally embrace the practice.

CHAPTER 6

GOD DOESN'T WANT ME MEDITATING

We've been talking about the barriers people build between themselves and meditation, but now I want to address one of the barriers that society tries to erect, which is the falsehood that meditation somehow conflicts with religion, especially Christianity.

Nothing could be further from the truth.

No matter what you might have heard, the practice of meditation is not a religion.

Nor is it a philosophy.

It is simply a technique to help you access the stillness inside of you. A technique, as I'll demonstrate in the next section, that is irrefutably rooted in neuroscience. So if you don't think there's anything "ungodly" about seeing a neurosurgeon, then you shouldn't think that there's anything "ungodly" about practicing meditation either.

Having said that, I do believe that meditation is an excellent way to build up and strengthen your relationship with God. As the Christian saint Padre Pio put it: "Through the study of books one seeks God; by meditation one finds him."

Indeed, every major religion teaches that good things arise from stillness. In Christianity, this state is called "Christ consciousness." In Islam, this state is referred to as *taqwa*, or "God conscious-ness." The yogis call it living in *samadhi*. In Buddhism, it's known as "nirvana." The Jews call it contemplation that can lead to *dveikus,* or "clinging to God." All the great prophets taught that you will find a sense of peace and purpose in stillness. It's the basic truth that connects all these different prophets who lived in different countries and walked the earth at different times during history. They all wanted you to be able to find peace within yourself.

Whether it was Buddha, Jesus Christ, or Muhammad, none of those prophets ever said that there was anything even remotely blasphemous about being still. Which is why I can't understand why the idea of sitting in stillness would feel threatening to any-one. The aim of any religion, or religious leader, should be to bring you closer to God, and there is no doubt that meditation does ex-actly that.

Let me keep it real with you right now. The *only* reason anyone could view meditation as a threat is because they are afraid of people making decisions from their heart and out of compassion. If you run a religious organization and you tell your congregation that meditation is blasphemous, then I have to assume you are threatened by the idea of their operating from their highest selves.

Maybe you don't want your flock to realize that the concepts of sexuality, race, and politics are nothing more than man-made distractions. Maybe you don't want them waking up and realizing they don't want to take part in the abuse of animals anymore. Just as there must be something threatening to you about the idea of people looking for peaceful and compassionate resolutions instead of going to war over those distractions. Think about that. What so-called religious authority could in *any* way be against a tool that can literally help build world peace? That's why anyone who suggests that God doesn't want people to meditate is a fraud who is lying to humanity.

Those are strong words, but I believe that when the stakes are this high, to paraphrase the late, great Biggie Smalls, I can't "bite my tongue for no one." One of the reasons I feel the stakes are so high is that more and more this religious stigma is being used to keep meditation from two groups who could really benefit from it: young people and prisoners.

Let's talk about young people first. I've been very fortunate to work with the director David Lynch's foundation, which has put a tremendous amount of time and money into bringing meditation into schools around the country. In particular, they've tried to help schools where a lot of the students come from disadvantaged and dysfunctional backgrounds.

One of those schools is the New Village Charter High School in Los Angeles, where Principal Javier Guzman has testified that out of all the measures they've introduced into the school to try to empower those kids, none has been as effective as meditation. Principal Guzman says that it was only through introducing meditation into his school that he was able to provide his students with a tool that taught them how to look past the tests, numbers, and percentages and begin to realize their potential as individuals. As one of Principal Guzman's students, a teenage mother, told him, "Quiet Time opened a door to someone I never knew I could be."

Another educator the David Lynch Foundation has worked with is Carlos A. Garcia, the former superintendent of the San Francisco school district. Mr. Garcia said he caught a lot of flak for introducing Quiet Time into that city's troubled public schools, but he said that there was no way he could pull back on the program. "We teach children about everything *but* themselves," he said at a symposium for the David Lynch Foundation that I also had the privilege of speaking at. "This is the only quiet time in their lives. . . . Meditation is transforming lives, neighborhoods, and it will transform our society."

Yet despite the impact meditation is having on these schools, educators like Principal Guzman and Superintendent Garcia are meeting resistance because there are still those in the community who feel meditation will somehow conflict with "Christian principles." Thankfully, many schools have figured out a way to get around that issue by relabeling meditation. Instead of saying that the kids need to spend fifteen minutes in meditation every day, they say they're spending it in "Quiet Time." If that's going to shut some of these critics up, so be it. Personally, I don't care what they call it as long as those kids are receiving this tool that is going to allow them to access the stillness inside of them.

We're also running up against similar prejudices in the prison system. Recently William E. Donaldson Correctional Facility in Alabama started a wonderful program in which prisoners were taught meditation as a way to cope with the stress and depression of being locked up. Stress that often erupts in terrible violence—William E. Donaldson was a corrections officer who was tragically killed at that prison back in 1990.

In the program, prisoners were taught a form of meditation called Vipassana, in which they focused on their breath. Prisoners in the program would wake up at four A.M. and meditate on and off until nine A.M., during which time they reflected on their lives and what they did to end up in prison. In a story that NPR did on the program, Johnny Mack Young, a sixty-one-year-old convicted murderer, said meditation allowed him for the first time in his life to really reflect on how he'd wound up going down the wrong path. In his case, he said he realized he'd never really confronted having been involved in the accidental death of his baby sister as a child. "That's one of the things that tortures me," Young said. "We learn this stuff. We learn it too late in life."

Young wasn't alone in reaping real benefits from meditation. The prison reported that inmates who participated in the program had a 20 percent reduction in disciplinary action after they learned to meditate.

But despite all that success, the prison was forced to cancel the program after chaplains in the state's prison system complained that it might not be "in keeping with Christian values." Thankfully, in this case the prison warden fought to bring the program back because he'd seen how much good it had done.

But that perception that meditation isn't "in keeping with Christian values" is still out there. Whether it's in schools or in prisons, there are still too many folks who are irrationally afraid of meditation. I don't get depressed about much, but I will admit I get sad thinking about how despite all the good we know that meditation does, we still face impediments in our society. The fact is, we owe the students in these overcrowded schools this quiet time. We owe their teachers too. How could we not share something so simple and free that we know brings grades up and takes violence down? That literally saves young people's lives? How can we deny them that?

You might not think we owe convicted murderers the right to meditate, but we certainly owe it to the guards who work with them. The guards who often pay the ultimate price for all that suppressed rage and depression.

It's not a popular view, but I feel we definitely owe it to the millions of people who have been needlessly locked up on drug offenses. People who for the most part only messed with drugs in the first place because they couldn't quiet the noise in their minds. Imagine how many of them could kick drugs for good if we taught them this method of quieting that noise and finding the serenity that they've been looking for in a bottle or a bag of crack. If we were really serious about ending the revolving-door prison system that the "War on Drugs" has created, there wouldn't be a better place to start than meditation.

I don't want to make it seem like I'm only beating up on Christians, or any other religious groups, either. That's because even outside religious groups there's still a perception that only weirdos or hippies practice meditation, that somehow it's not a practice for "normal" folks.

So to anyone reading this who might still feel the influence of that perception, I urge you to open up your heart and mind to the concept of meditation. Experience it for yourself before you make any sort of judgment about it.

I'm glad I didn't allow that perception to cloud my lenses. On the surface, meditation would seem alien to an African-American who grew up Christian in Hollis, Queens. But I've found that it comes effortlessly to me, like it's part of my DNA. Certainly easier than learning how to drive a car after living in New York City my whole life. And no matter what neighborhood or city or country you come from, you'll have a similar reaction. As David

Lynch says, "People think meditation is weird now, but in the future the weird people are going to be the ones that DON'T meditate."

I want us to reach that future faster. One of the primary reasons I'm writing this guide is because I want to help propel meditation into the mainstream where it belongs. It's really very similar to the type of service I've tried to provide throughout my career—helping guide ideas or movements that are being unfairly ignored out of the underground and into the light, where everyone can appreciate them. I was able to serve in that role with rap music, hip-hop fashion, and spoken-word poetry, and I hope to be able to serve meditation in a similar role. Because despite the incredible impact hip-hop has had in America—and I believe it's done nothing short of transforming race relations not only in this country, but around the world—I believe that meditation can have an even greater impact!

I'll even go as far as to say that I believe that meditation can help bring about world peace. That's a bold statement, but I know it to be true. And remember, I'm not your typical "hippie." I've seen dysfunction in both rich and poor people firsthand, and I'm very aware of what people can be like when they're operating from their lower levels. But I also know that if we can collectively settle our minds and bodies through meditation, then we can collectively raise our minds and bodies to their highest possibilities.

Maybe that sounds weird. Or naïve. Or even blasphemous. But

to me, that higher state is actually our natural one as humans. So the question becomes not whether or not that world can exist, but rather, how can we speed up the process by which we bring it about? And the answer, no matter whether you're a Christian, Jew, Hindu, or atheist, is through meditation.

CHAPTER 7

WHETHER YOU LIKE IT OR NOT

A final thought on overcoming whatever barriers you feel are preventing you from meditating:

You are already moving toward stillness.

Whether you like it or not.

I don't say that as a threat or as a warning, but rather as an observation on the basic nature of human evolution. As we grow older, we start to see the world more clearly. We become more aware of how distracted we've been, of how we've often failed to appreciate all of the beauty and wonder around us.

How many people, as they near the end of their lives, do you think look back and say, "You know, I wish I'd spent more time at the office." Or "If I could do it all over again, I'd have spent more time on my couch watching TV and less time going out into the world and exploring."

Not too many.

Do you think that when a rich guy is on his deathbed, he sighs and says, "Wow, if I could only drive my sports car one last time . . ."? Or "If I could just get out of this bed, I'd go put on all my gold watches." Of course not. He might wish he could go back in time and push his daughter on a swing again or have his son on his lap while he reads him a book one last time. But the material stuff, no matter how much he accumulated, won't be on his mind.

No, when it is time to get put in that box, most of us have finally realized that a happy, contented life isn't one spent focused on building wealth or collecting toys. Instead, we finally see that true happiness lies in being compassionate and appreciating the world, rather than being coldhearted and greedy. We realize that our favorite moments were those spent simply with the people we loved, the moments we spent walking on the beach on a beautiful day, hearing the waves and feeling the sun on our faces. Or simply sitting with our friends and laughing at a good joke.

In short, we all eventually come to understand that our happiness is derived from being present in the moment. In seeing the miracles that are constantly unfolding around us every second, instead of blindly running past them.

All I'm really asking you in this book is, "Why not speed up that process? Why not get there sooner than later? Why not start enjoying and deriving happiness from the world every day, instead of only in brief flashes?"

So if you've been holding on to any of these misconceptions

about meditation—that you don't have time, that it's too hard and you can't do it right, that you don't have anywhere to do it, or that it's "ungodly"—please let go of all those fears right now.

Because if you're afraid of any of those things, what you're really saying is that you're afraid of your own mind.

Which might not be such a crazy thing to feel. Our minds, especially when we don't maintain them, can be a pretty scary place. When you let years'—even decades'—worth of fear, prejudice, disappointment, rejection, anger, and heartbreak pile up in there, it's no wonder you don't want to start poking around too much.

But the bottom line is, your mind isn't going anywhere. You're going to have to live in there not only every day, but also every second of every day. And unlike a house or even a computer's hard drive, there's no limit to the amount of junk you can pile up. You can keep tossing anxiety and distractions in there until the day you die.

But why live like that? Instead of creeping around "afraid of the dark" in your own mind, use meditation to help pull back the drapes, open up the windows, and let some light in for once.

And once all that light begins to pour in and that fresh air begins to circulate, you're going to feel great. You're going to see that for all the anxiety you put yourself through, there was really nothing to be afraid of all along. Because despite whatever you've been through, or whatever you've thought over the years, your mind is a fundamentally good place. Your mind, once all the junk gets cleared out, only has happy and contented thoughts in it.

Remember, there are no barriers preventing you from reacquainting yourself with that mind. It's the distractions that are making you anxious, not what's in your heart and in your mind!

Let those fears go and claim the happiness that's always been inside of you. That is your birthright.

PART THREE

The Physical Benefits of Meditation

CHAPTER 8

CHANGE YOUR BRAIN,
CHANGE YOUR LIFE

Now that we've gotten past those barriers that you thought were separating you from meditation, it's time to get into some of the concrete ways that meditation will benefit your life. And as you'll see, there are many more benefits than perceived barriers!

Specifically, I want to discuss the positive physical effects meditation will have on your brain. I said what I'm promoting in this book is science. And now I'm about to prove it.

Some of it might get a little technical, but it's important to show that there are concrete physical benefits from meditation. It's very important to understand that scientists are learning that when you spend time in stillness every day, it *will* dramatically change how your brain operates.

In addition to how it will impact the physical makeup of your brain, I also want to address the incredible benefits meditation will have on your physical health. From lowering your blood pressure and stress levels to decreasing your chances of suffering heart disease and even helping you eat healthier, meditation can play a huge role in helping you feel better and live longer!

TWO PARTS TO THE BRAIN

I want to start by talking about meditation's effect on the brain because despite its being the part of the body we use the most every day, most of us have very little knowledge on how our brains actually work.

Sometimes, and for many years I was guilty of this myself, we make the mistake of thinking our brains are formless spaces in which ideas just float around. Or if we do think of our brains in a physical sense, it's only as a big lump of gray gook.

To use a political analogy, one pet peeve I have is that many people tend to refer to Africa as a country. It's always, "In Africa they need to do this," or "In Africa they should do that." But the truth is that Africa is made up of many different countries, cultures, languages, and perspectives. There are many, many layers to Africa. If you only view it as a single entity, then you're never going to truly understand it.

Well, the same is true of your brain. You might only think of it as that featureless gray blob, but it actually has many different parts and layers, each with its own function and impact on your thinking and body. Which is why if you only think of your brain as formless space, you're never going to be able to use it to its full potential.

Obviously I'm not a doctor, and you probably didn't pick up this book looking for a neurology lesson, so I'm going to try not to get too technical here. I do, however, want to break down two very important parts of your brain, so that you can begin to get a better sense of how your emotions are generated and in turn how you can begin to use meditation to have better control over them.

The first is the cerebrum, which is the largest part of your brain and is divided into right and left hemispheres. The left hemisphere is primarily where linear, logical, and language-based thinking takes place. To put it more plainly, if the left side of your cerebrum were a person, it'd be someone who's very logical and rational, like Mr. Spock from *Star Trek*. This is why we see a lot of so-called left-brain types go into professions that focus more on following instructions and patterns than creativity, like science or accounting.

The right hemisphere, conversely, is where your nonlinear and emotional thinking takes place. If that side were a person, it'd be more like the comedian Robin Williams or the rapper DMX— someone who gives off a lot of uncensored emotion and energy.

Which is why when we talk about "right-brain" people, we're usually talking about creative types who have an affinity for art, music, and writing. The type of folk the world might call "free thinkers."

In fact, the reason why young children are so emotional is

because they mainly use that right side of their brains. It's not until around the age of eight that we begin to show a preference for one side or the other.

Now, here's the thing: Even though the two sides of our cerebrum are physically connected by a bridge, known as the corpus callosum, as we grow older, we stop utilizing it. The creative ideas tend to stay on the right side, while the structured and orderly ideas tend to stay on the left.

Obviously there's nothing wrong with being a creative, right-side type. Just as there's nothing wrong with being a logical, structured, left-side type. But no matter what type you are, wouldn't you like to tap into that underused side just a little bit more?

If you're a creative thinker, you'd still probably like to have a little more order in your life. Just as if you're an accountant who loves figuring out the bottom line, you still might like to have more creative flashes than you normally do.

One of the great benefits of meditation is that it helps you start using that bridge between your right and left sides again. We know this because recently the UCLA Laboratory of Neuro Imaging conducted a study using diffusion tensor imaging, or DTI (which is sort of like an MRI), to look at the structural connectivity of the brain. And they found that the corpus callosum was more connected with the right and left hemispheres in meditators than in people who didn't meditate. In other words, it's almost like growing old builds a wall around your corpus callosum and meditation helps knock it down.

So by just sitting in silence every day, your tendency to lean heavily toward either the right or left side of your brain will slowly begin to come back into balance. And when that balance returns, it's sort of like being a kid again. When it felt just as natural to spend an hour working on your handwriting as it did to spend an hour playing dress-up and pretending that you were a pirate. When you didn't feel so disorganized and scatterbrained, just as you didn't feel creatively shackled.

And when you begin to experience that childlike ability to be several things at once, it's incredibly liberating. I can remember, during my first few months of meditating, being surprised that sometimes after I was done I would find myself giggling like a little kid. Not because anything particularly funny had happened, but because I just felt childlike and free again. I'm pretty silly by nature, so at first I just chalked it up to general goofiness. But now I know what I was feeling wasn't a fluke or a coincidence. It was my brain starting to fire up parts of itself that had been underutilized for years.

To put it another way, when you start to connect those two sides of your brain again, it's almost like meeting an old friend after many years. Except the old friend is *you*. Instinctively you knew that creative thinker, or organized person, was always somewhere in you, you just didn't know where to find them. Meditation can reintroduce you to that part of yourself that's been "missing" for so long.

FIXING YOUR BRAIN'S ALARM SYSTEM

Meditation also has a powerful impact on what's known as your limbic brain. It's the part of your brain where your most basic emotions are generated, in particular your fight-or-flight responses.

"Guarding" the front of your limbic brain is a smaller, almond-shaped structure called the amygdala. Its job is to assess every new situation you encounter and then tell your limbic brain whether it's dangerous or not.

To use an analogy, think of your limbic brain as a car owner and the amygdala as a car alarm system. Every time the car alarm detects what it perceives to be a threat, it's going to go off and make a lot of noise. Then it's up to the owner to decide if he's just going to deactivate the alarm and go back to sleep or actually get up and investigate.

Here's where the trouble starts: Every time your amygdala sounds its alarm, your limbic brain begins releasing stress hormones like adrenaline and cortisol. These are secretions that create a sense of fear and anxiety in your body. Those are important senses to have when you're facing a truly life-threatening situation. If someone is about to rob you on the street or an animal is about to attack you in the woods, you want those secretions to be telling your body, "It's time to get out of here. Run!"

But they also come with a price. Extremely powerful, those hormones are also extremely toxic and stay in your body for several days after they're released. Which is why you only want your body to be releasing them when it's absolutely necessary.

So the question becomes, how can we train our amygdala to help distinguish between what's just annoying and what's truly life threatening? To continue the analogy, to stop being one of those car alarms that goes off every time there's a storm or someone drives by playing loud music and instead only go off when someone is really trying to steal your ride?

The answer, you probably won't be surprised to hear, is through meditation.

By slowing down our pace and allowing our thoughts to come at us much more slowly, meditation gives our amygdala a chance to make more calm and measured assessments of situations.

For example, consider someone cutting in front of you in a line or swooping in at the last second and stealing a parking spot you've been waiting for. Those situations aren't at all life threatening, but they'd still cause your brain to release adrenaline and cortisol, right? And in some of you, they produce so much adrenaline that you'll literally fly into a homicidal rage.

But is the annoyance of losing a parking spot, or your place in line, really worth releasing toxins into your body? Or course not. You'll find another parking spot or get into that movie in a few minutes anyway. But you'll be stuck with those toxins for a long time.

When your mind is calm, however, instead of telling our limbic brain to release its toxins, your amygdala will say, "Yes, I didn't like what just happened, but it's not worth sounding the alarm. Let this one slide."

Now imagine if just five times a day you were able to let a perceived slight or dis go instead of reacting negatively to it. That instead of beginning to seethe when a coworker made a snide little comment, or slamming a door when you see that your son never cleaned up his room like you told him to, you were able to just shrug those moments off. To accept them without investing any energy in them.

That would mean that five times a day you wouldn't be needlessly releasing toxic chemicals into your body. Think of how much better you would feel after just one week. Think about how much less tension your body would be carrying. Think about how much clearer your mind would be.

Wouldn't that be a much freer way to live?

MORE RELAXED

Another wonderful physical benefit of meditation is that it helps relax your mind. Especially if, like me, you sometimes struggle to get enough sleep. We've known that meditation produces deep restfulness since the 1970s, when a cardiologist named Dr. Herbert Benson conducted a study at Harvard where he measured the blood pressure, brain waves, and body temperatures of people meditating. He found that while they were meditating they used 17 percent less oxygen, lowered their heart rates by three beats a minute, and decreased their beta brain waves, while increasing their alpha and theta brain waves, during sleep. Based on those findings, Dr. Benson concluded that the rest people receive during meditation is often as deep or even deeper than what they might experience during sleep.

The reason he came to that conclusion was largely because of the impact meditation had on brain waves. Whether we're awake or sleeping, there are always electronic signals pulsing through our brains known as beta, alpha, delta, theta, and gamma waves. Beta waves are usually associated with goal-oriented tasks and problem solving, while alpha and theta waves are associated with restfulness. And delta waves are normally most active during sleep.

What Dr. Benson found, and what has been backed up in a recent study conducted by the University of Sydney in Australia, is that when we meditate, our beta waves decrease. This means that when you meditate, the part of your brain that is always working on making plans and solving problems—in other words, stressing— finally gets to take a break.

This is a critical point because a lot of people make the mistake of thinking that when they sleep, they are somehow "turning off" their mind. But after you go to sleep, those beta waves are still zipping back and forth in your brain. They're even darting around during REM (rapid eye movement) sleep, which is considered the "deepest" part of sleep.

Have you ever been stressed out over something and gone to bed early, thinking that "a good night's sleep" will solve everything, but when you wake up eight hours later, you still feel stressed and anxious? Well, you can thank those beta waves. Because even though your body was resting during the night, your mind wasn't. It was still going through its paces, still trying to figure shit out and cook up strategies to "deal" with your life.

By turning down those beta waves, meditation is essentially letting your "thinking mind" take a break from itself. If that weren't enough, it's also increasing your theta and alpha waves, which promote deep relaxation.

This is why meditation can help you feel relaxed and focused even when you have trouble sleeping. Personally, I once went through a stage where I struggled with insomnia. Before I found meditation, I used to stay up at night thinking about not only what I perceived to be problems from the day that had just passed but also what I thought would be problems in the day to come.

But as I grew a little older and also wiser, thanks to meditation and yoga, I started to understand that dwelling in the past and the future is a fundamental cause of suffering. And once I learned to live in the present, instead of the past or the future, then my sleep became much more restful.

Today, I still have occasional bouts of insomnia, but I've learned to accept it and not get hung up over a night or two of restlessness. If I've only gotten a few hours of sleep the night before, I still meditate the next morning, and I always feel refreshed afterward. Even when my body might be tired or dragging, my mind still feels sharp.

YOU *CAN* RETRAIN YOUR BRAIN

When we talk about fixing our brain's "alarm system," creating better balance through reconnecting its right and left sides, or decreasing beta waves, we're making a very fundamental assertion: that we *are* able to change our brains. A physical change that is going to promote emotional and spiritual happiness.

This shouldn't exactly be breaking news. From the time of Buddha, the yogis have taught that you can improve your emotional and mental state by practicing meditation. They might not have had neuroimaging to "prove" it, but thousands of years ago the yogis knew that meditation had this effect on your brain. Just like Jesus knew it too. But for better or worse, it hasn't been till the last few decades that Western doctors have finally caught up to the science behind this ancient truth.

One of the biggest misconceptions in Western medicine about our brains was that as we get older, they lose their ability to grow. The prevailing wisdom was that our brains reach their peak during adulthood and then everything starts to go downhill the older we get. While that unfortunately might still hold true with the rest of our body, the good news is that scientists are beginning to discover that with the help of meditation, our brains can keep growing right into old age.

Dr. Eileen Luders, a professor at UCLA who helped run the study I mentioned earlier, recently told the medical journal *Neuro-Image,* "Regular use [of meditation] may strengthen the connections between neurons and can also make new connections," and "these tiny changes, in thousands of connections, can lead to visible changes in the structure of the brain."

Dr. Luders says that their study found not only that meditation helped people's corpus callosum (that bridge between the brain's right and left sides) grow, but that it also promoted positive growth in the gray matter.

Why is increased gray matter so significant? Because gray matter is one of the most important parts of your brain—the cells that make up your gray matter are responsible for your memory, sense of self, attention, and empathy. That's why while 20 percent of the oxygen that comes into your body gets sent to your brain, once it's there 95 percent of that oxygen gets routed directly to your gray matter.

It's known that gray matter plays a critical role in development: Studies have found that children with autism, or who have sadly been abused or severely neglected as young children, have significantly less gray matter in their brains.

So to know that meditation can help build up gray matter, even decades after scientists previously thought it would have stopped growing, is tremendous news.

And the scientists at UCLA aren't the only ones coming to this conclusion. Recently a team of researchers at Massachusetts General Hospital used MRIs to study the brains of people who had recently started meditating and found that even after just several weeks, their gray matter had begun thickening.

If you get a chance, try to check out Professor Hedy Kober's TEDx talk about meditation on YouTube. She starts it off with the announcement that she has bad news and good news: "The bad news is that shit happens," she says.

"The good news is that each and every one of you has the power to control and change your experience of this shit when it happens. You can learn and train yourself to have a better attitude about it." And her prescribed method for making that change? Meditation.

"Practitioners have long claimed that meditation also provides cognitive and psychological benefits that persist throughout the day," Dr. Sara Lazar, the study's senior author, told *ScienceDaily*. "This study demonstrates that changes in brain structure may underlie some of these reported improvements and that people are not just feeling better because they are spending time relaxing."

Another scientist, Richard Davidson of the University of Wisconsin, found similar results in a study he did on Tibetan monks who were master meditators. "What we found is that the longtime practitioners showed brain activation on a scale we have never seen before," he told *The Washington Post*. "Their mental practice is having an effect on the brain in the same way golf or tennis practice will enhance performance."

And Yale University psychiatry professor Hedy Kober recently gave an incredible TEDx talk in Buenos Aires, where she described a study she and other Yale researchers conducted on the link between meditation and our brains. After studying how meditation affected the way people experience the stress of nicotine withdrawal, Kober said she and her colleagues concluded that "learning how to meditate can significantly alter your experience of stress and can change not only the way your brain functions during stress, but also the way it's structured over time." Kober added that the study convinced them that the brain "is not made of plastic like a bucket, but rather that like plastic it can be molded into different shapes."

So to put all this in layman's terms, meditation is going to help build up the part of your brain that promotes memory and emotion and help shrink that part that causes stress. Even at an age where you've been taught that not only has your brain stopped growing, but that it's on its way downhill.

As I'm going to discuss in greater detail shortly, I doubt anyone reading this book has killed more of their brain cells than I have. During my teens, twenties, and even thirties, I smoked a ton of angel dust. There aren't many drugs that do more damage to your brain than dust. Considering how much cocaine, marijuana, and angel dust I put into my body over the years, I should barely be functioning by this point in my life.

Yet here I am in my fifties and my mind feels as sharp and as focused as it ever has. And I know it's because of meditation. I might not have known before I started researching this book that it was because my gray matter is growing and my amygdala isn't getting overworked, but I could still *feel* it. Even after only a few months of meditating.

That's why if you only take one message from this book, let it be this—you are not "stuck" with the brain that you have right now.

As Dr. Davidson said, just like you can change your body through a consistent physical regimen, we now know that you can change the shape of your brain through the consistent practice of meditation.

I don't care if you've been stressed out for years or have been smoking pot every night since you were thirteen years old—you can still change your brain through meditation if you want to!

Some people like to call meditation "push-ups for your brain." And while I hope you'll leave this book seeing that there's a lot more to it than that, it's not a bad analogy. Just as you know that if you do push-ups every day you're going to have bigger muscles in a couple of weeks, it's no different with your brain and meditation.

If you put in those twenty minutes twice a day, your brain is going to start growing in the areas that are helpful and shrink in those that can be harmful. I'm telling you this, the scientists are starting to tell you this, and the yogis have been telling people this for thousands of years. All you have to do is accept it and start the practice.

HELPING TEENAGERS PUT ON THE BRAKES

Earlier I was talking about the incredible impact meditation has been having in schools, especially those that experience a lot of reckless behavior and "acting out." Now I want to explain in scientific terms exactly why meditation does so much to help these young people cope with the stress of being a teenager.

If you think cell phones, the Internet, and social media are distracting to adults, imagine what teenagers are experiencing today. Personally, AM radio, some 45 records, a few comic books, and a handful of TV channels were enough for me growing up. But today kids are growing up with hundreds of video channels, thousands of songs, cameras, and countless social media sites just on their *phones*. To say nothing of what's on their TV sets, computers, or gaming systems. Sure, I got distracted as a kid, but I also had quiet moments to balance it out. Before I moved to Hollis, we lived in Jamaica, Queens, and back then there were woods near our house that had a lot of snakes in them. I actually used to spend hours searching for snakes and even developed a little reputation as the only kid in the neighborhood who wasn't afraid to pick them up and play with them. When I got older, there weren't any snakes in Hollis (or at least not that kind), but I would spend hours sitting in the room I shared with my brother Joey, listening to records by R & B groups I loved like Blue Magic, the Spinners, and the Delfonics.

Today, it would be very hard to find those sorts of moments. Instead of wandering around the woods looking for snakes, I'd probably be in front of a TV playing video games. Or instead of lying on a bed with my eyes closed listening to records, I'd be sitting in front of my computer listening to songs in my headphones while I simultaneously texted my friends, updated my Twitter, and updated my

Facebook profile. Instead of getting lost in the music, I'd barely be paying attention to it.

Those calm, focused moments are very hard for teenagers to find today. It's like they are being raised in the middle of Times Square, under constant barrage from a never-ending stream of sights and sounds.

But if we're going to allow our children to spend hours watching TV, surfing the net, and sending text messages, then we have to give them something to counterbalance all that frantic energy. Something to block out the noise and help them refocus on what's inside of them.

Think of life as like an ocean of consciousness. When young people experience it primarily through screens (TVs, computers, phones, etc.), they're never straying too far from the surface of that ocean. What we need to do is teach them how to go past the surface and begin to experience life at its depths.

That's because every level of stillness contains more and more peace. More and more happiness. We want to teach our teenagers that instead of always floating on the surface, they should be like one of those old-fashioned bell divers with the glass mask and air hose, slowly sinking down to the bottom of the ocean. The deeper the diver goes, the more happiness he's going to encounter. So when he finally comes back up to the surface, he's going to bring a true treasure back with him: pure bliss and happiness.

Again, this is the treasure we must share with our young people. Because if we don't, they are always going to be stuck at the surface.

Always stuck checking that screen instead of looking within. Always stuck listening to what their friends, peers, or screens tell them, instead of what they know to be true in their hearts.

Every young person needs to learn meditation. I don't care if your kids go to your local public high school, a difficult school in the hood, or a fancy boarding school—if they're constantly IM-ing, texting, Skyping, or whatever else is going to be hot by the time you read this, then they need some quiet time through meditation.

We've seen that meditation helps grow the gray matter of the brain, and this is especially significant when it comes to teenagers. I learned this after I had heard a lecture sponsored by the David Lynch Foundation with Dr. Richard Friedman of Weill Cornell Medical College, who explained how meditation can actually slow down teenagers' tendency to get themselves into life-threatening situations.

According to Dr. Friedman, one of the quirks of human development is that regions of the brain develop at different rates. This is especially true of the nucleus, or reward center of the brain, which drives risky behavior like sex, gambling, shoplifting, speeding in cars, accepting dares, etc. Basically all the wild stuff that teenagers do that drives us adults crazy and gets them into so much trouble.

Unfortunately, the nucleus develops faster than the rest of our brain, though there's a good reason for it. Young people need to take the risk of leaving the nest, the safety of living with their parents, and strike out on their own in the world. If that nucleus didn't develop so quickly, young people wouldn't feel as compelled to create their own lives.

The issue is that the prefrontal cortex, which is the reasoning part of our brains, doesn't develop nearly as quickly. So while our nucleus might be fully functioning at fifteen, our prefrontal cortex doesn't really come into its own until our midtwenties.

What this means in layman's terms is that between fifteen and twenty-five, our brains are good at taking risks but not so good at being reasonable.

Or to use Dr. Friedman's even simpler analogy, it's like teenagers are cars with fully developed accelerators and underdeveloped brakes.

And as all teachers and parents can tell you, there are few things more frustrating, and dangerous, than a teenager who knows how to use his accelerator but not his brakes.

The good news is that in his studies, Dr. Friedman found that meditation helps teenagers develop their brakes much quicker. By increasing the gray matter in the prefrontal cortex, meditation allows teenagers to bridge the gap that normally exists between the risk-taking and reasoning parts of their brain.

What this means is that a teenager who in the past might have taken that dare to push their car up to one hundred miles an hour on a straightaway, or shoplift a dress, or even take a gun to school, won't be as prone to making that foolish decision after learning how to meditate. When they feel the impulse to do something crazy, instead of putting the pedal to the metal, they might actually tap the brakes a few times instead.

My daughters are just becoming teenagers now, and you can best believe I make sure they meditate every day, most of the time with me. They've actually already been meditating for several years and there's no doubt that it's changed their lives dramatically for the better. Part of it's due to the increased compassion and focus it's brought them, but the ability to slow down and be calm when everyone else about them is speeding up is a large part of it too. As a parent, it's always tough to send kids out in the world and worry that they may get caught up in something dangerous or harmful. Knowing that my kids are meditators gives me confidence that no matter what situations they find themselves in, especially as they grow older, they're going to approach them from a calm and controlled space as opposed to a reckless and distracted one.

CHAPTER 9

HOW MEDITATION HELPS
YOUR BODY

While meditation's benefits for your brain alone should be enough to get anyone to sit down and start the practice, I want to highlight some of the incredible things meditation can do for the rest of your body too.

I've spoken about stress a few times already, but I want to point out here that stress isn't just an emotional condition. Remember, stress is what activates your fight-or-flight response, which is in turn what sends all those powerful toxins into your bloodstream.

So while you might think of stress as a mood that you sometimes go through, the fact is that it is having very negative physical effects on your body. Or to put it even plainer, stress will make you physically sick. And eventually kill you.

One of the most common ways that stress breaks us down physically is through high blood pressure. When you are constantly stressed out and anxious, it causes your blood pressure to rise. And once that happens, you become less likely to exercise and more likely to overeat.

Soon you find yourself in a vicious cycle that more often than not leads to deadly conditions like strokes and heart disease. In fact, the Centers for Disease Control estimates that 69 percent of people who have a first heart attack, 77 percent of people who have a first stroke, and 74 percent of people with chronic heart failure have high blood pressure. So while it's tempting to pass high blood pressure off as one of the realities of modern life, the cold truth is that heart disease is the leading cause of death in America, killing over half a million people every year.

It's especially deadly in the African-American community, where, according to the US Department of Health and Human Services, people are 40 percent more likely to develop high blood pressure than in other ethnic groups. And it's really a stone-cold killer for black women, who the DHHS estimates are 30 percent more likely to die from heart disease than white men.

Thankfully, meditation has been proven to be extremely effective at reversing that cycle. The National Institutes of Health, the American Medical Association, the American Heart Association, the Mayo Clinic, and scientists from Harvard and Stanford have all stated that meditation can reduce stress and high blood pressure. A recent study by Dr. Norman Rosenthal, a world-renowned psychiatrist and author who works with the David Lynch Foundation, even found that people who practice meditation are 30 percent less likely to die from heart disease.

His findings were backed up in a recent study published in the journal *Circulation: Cardiovascular Quality and Outcomes,* in which a group of people with coronary heart disease were asked to take a class on Transcendental Meditation (TM) (more about TM later). Over the next five years the group experienced a 48 percent reduction in the risk of heart attack, stroke, and death.

Based on all these findings, some insurance companies are starting to reimburse people with high blood pressure for Transcendental Meditation instruction. I've spoken to Dr. Rosenthal about this and he told me that it's a very important development in terms of how we treat heart disease in this country.

Think about it: Right now, if you develop high blood pressure, how do you get treated? You're told to cut down on salt, exercise more, and start taking a pill like Lopressor or Prinivil. Pills that are going to cost you thousands of dollars each year and potentially create side effects like insomnia, fatigue, depression, dizziness, and erectile dysfunction. Pills that, once you are on them, you are probably going to have to stay on for the rest of your life!

But with meditation, there aren't any prescriptions you have to pay for every month. Just as there aren't any side effects. If anything, meditation not only lowers your blood pressure but also makes you more rested! (I haven't seen any studies yet, but I can tell you that it certainly doesn't cause erectile dysfunction. In fact, research has suggested that meditation can help reverse erectile dysfunction. So meditation is not only saving lives, it's creating new ones too!)

So before you become one of the one in three Americans who develop high blood pressure, give meditation a try. Instead of committing to a pill cooked up by a big pharmaceutical company, commit to taking two twenty-minute mini vacations every day. Mini vacations that are proven to make you 30 percent less likely to meet up with the most aggressive killer out there. Let that sink in—meditation is going to give you a 30 percent better chance than the rest of the population to beat the number one killer in the country! Who wouldn't want those odds?

CHANGE YOUR CELLS FOR THE BETTER

While the statistics for meditation's effectiveness for lowering high blood pressure are really encouraging, I want to mention a couple of other areas where research is finding that meditation is very effective in improving our health.

In 2013, a study by the University of California found that men with prostate cancer who started practicing meditation, exercising, and following a vegetarian diet (which I highly recommend also!) were able to rejuvenate their damaged cells.

Specifically, on a cellular level we all have little protective caps on our chromosomes called telomeres. (Kind of like those little caps at the ends of your shoelaces that keep them from coming apart.) When those cell caps start to separate, it's a message to your body that the cells are no longer healthy and are ready to die. Which is why a lot of scientists believe there is a connection between shortened telomeres and deadly cell diseases like cancer.

But when the University of California scientists checked in on men who had been meditating, after just five months they found that their telomere length had increased significantly, by an average of 10 percent.

In announcing their findings, Professor Dean Ornish said that he believed that it wasn't an exaggeration that meditation could actually fight cancer. "These comprehensive lifestyle changes may significantly reduce the risk of a wide variety of diseases and premature mortality," he wrote. "Our genes, and our telomeres, are a predisposition, but they are not necessarily our fate."

Studies are also finding that meditation is very effective in calming our nervous systems. According to an article published by the medical journal *The Lancet Oncology*, the practice of meditation does work "related to activating the parasympathetic and quieting the sympathetic nervous system."

In other words, meditation can help increase the flow of your blood and digestive juices (parasympathetic), while at the same time keeping your breathing and heart rate low (sympathetic), which is where you want them to be.

And while noting that studies are still inconclusive, the Mayo Clinic has identified several other physical ailments that seemed to be improved by meditation, including allergies, asthma, pain, substance abuse, and binge eating (more on those last two shortly).

MEDITATION AND YOUR DIET

Chances are you probably spend a good deal of time worrying about your weight. The percentages vary from year to year, but generally over half of the country is on a diet at any given time. Yet studies show that almost 80 percent of people who do lose weight on one of those diets end up gaining it back.

If you've ever experienced that kind of "yo-yo" dieting, then you know how deflating it can be. You pour a tremendous amount of energy into exercise and regulating the types of foods you eat. After you reach whatever goal you set for yourself, you go out and buy some new clothes and get to spend a couple of weeks, or maybe even months, enjoying the "new" you.

But in time your ability to watch what you eat starts to fade and your commitment to exercise starts to waver. Soon the pounds start to pile back on and before you know it, it's time to put those "new you" pants in the closet and pull out your old "fat clothes."

When that happens, it can become very easy to give up all hope that you'll ever lose weight again. After all, you did everything you were supposed to do, but it just didn't stick. "I guess," a lot of people tell themselves, "I'm just always going to be fat."

But what I'm here to tell you is that you *can* change the basic nature of your relationship with food through meditation.

That's because when you meditate, you will become much more mindful of not only the food you put in your body but how it actually tastes while you're eating it. Thinking about food might not seem like a way to lose weight—after all, we've been conditioned to believe that the only way to do that is to either starve yourself on a diet or exercise like a crazy person.

But more and more experts, including my good friends Deepak Chopra and Dr. Oz, are starting to recommend meditation as a way to access the "mindful eating" habits that will help you lose weight once and for all.

So instead of getting trapped in that cycle of losing weight when you're on a diet and gaining it right back once you go off it, you can have a much more healthy and balanced approach to what you eat. An approach that will allow you to eat all sorts of different foods, but in much healthier portions. And perhaps more important, a relationship in which you sit down to eat when you are physically hungry, as opposed to emotionally hungry. Because as Deepak puts it, "There are two reasons people put food in their bodies. One is they are physically hungry. The other is they are emotionally hungry. And if you put food in your body to satisfy your emotional hunger, you're going to gain weight."

Let me be very clear here—I'm not saying that when you start meditating the pounds are just going to magically start falling off of you. Instead, what I'm suggesting is that as you spend more and more time in stillness, the distractions that have you making poor choices when it comes to food will start to slip away. And as you become more conscious of those choices, you'll feel more empowered to change them.

Instead of helping you embark on a diet, meditation will help you embark on a lifestyle change. It's going to help you reexamine your entire relationship with food and learn how to stop being controlled by what your body thinks it needs or what society is telling you to crave.

REGULATING HOW MUCH YOU EAT

So what exactly is "mindful eating"? And how is it going to help you lose weight?

Essentially, mindful eating is the practice of slowing down and savoring each bite of your food, instead of eating it unconsciously. In mindful eating, when you bite into a piece of food, you stay focused on how it smells, how it tastes, its texture and its color.

That might seem like very simplistic advice—after all, who doesn't know what their food tastes like or smells like? But if we're being honest, the answer is most of us.

That's because we've become conditioned in this country to eat our food distractedly. And you know what I'm talking about. How many times have you eaten your dinner in front of the TV or while you were reading a magazine? Or had a snack while you were talking on the phone? Or even driving your car?

Probably pretty often. And when you eat that way, you're not truly experiencing the food that you're putting in your mouth. Sure, you might taste the first bite or two of that sandwich or piece of cake, but after a few minutes your thoughts get so wrapped up in that TV show or the conversation that you're having with your friend that you can look down and suddenly there's an empty plate in front of you and you can barely remember what that food even tasted like.

When you eat that way, not only are you robbing yourself of the pleasure of experiencing just how good a piece of pie can taste, but you're also making it more likely that you'll eat more pie than you really need. Because if you eat a piece of pie to sate a hunger, especially an emotional one, if you don't even remember eating it, what are you going to do once you're finished? Eat some more.

And that's how you find yourself bingeing and wolfing down a whole pie, tub of ice cream, or box of cookies without even knowing it.

Eating without thinking about what you're putting in your mouth might seem like a silly thing to do, but we're actually encouraged to eat that way. Think about what sort of foods you're usually eating when you binge. It usually isn't healthy foods like strawberries or eggplant or brown rice. No, when you start shoveling down food without thinking about it, it's usually processed foods.

I'm talking about ice cream, cookies, potato chips, candy, pretzels, sugary cereals—the omnipresent snacks that it seems so hard to say no to. And you know why saying no seems so hard? It's not because those processed sweet or fatty foods truly taste so good, but because they've been genetically engineered to make you crave them. That's right, the big food companies literally have teams of scientists whose only job is to try to figure out ways to make you crave these products. This should be illegal, but instead it's happening in plain sight.

An award-winning reporter for *The New York Times* named Michael Moss recently wrote an excellent—and disturbing—book on this called *Salt Sugar Fat: How the Food Giants Hooked Us*. In the book, Moss talks about how scientists have perfected the "bliss point" in many of these products. The "bliss point" is the perfect amount of sugar that will give you a high and get you hooked on a type of cookie or cereal.

Moss also writes about how those scientists have perfected what the industry calls "mouth feel." You might not know the term, but you definitely know the "feel"—that warm, satisfying sensation you experience when you bite into melted cheese or some crispy fried chicken. Unfortunately, "mouth feel" comes from super-high levels of fat, which create the same high that sugar does but come with even more calories.

Remember, these addictive qualities aren't a coincidence. These foods have been developed and marketed by the food giants to get you hooked. As Moss told *Time* magazine, "In some ways getting unhooked on [processed] foods is harder than getting unhooked on narcotics, because you can't go cold turkey. You can't just stop eating. The head of the National Institute on Drug Abuse in Washington says that it's more difficult for people to control their eating habits than narcotics. She is hugely empathic with overeaters."

Not to be too dramatic, but every time you walk into a supermarket, especially the center aisles where the popular salty and sugary items are always stocked, you're basically under attack. Hundreds of millions of dollars have been spent so that you will not only buy an item that's unhealthy for you but also keep coming back for it time and time again.

So the question becomes, since the food giants are pushing these products that are so difficult to eat in moderation, how can we change our relationship with what we eat? Instead of gorging on sugary, fatty, and salty foods, how can we learn to eat smaller portions but still get that enjoyment that we've come to associate with those processed foods? And the answer, many researchers are discovering, is through meditation.

For instance, Professor Jean Kristeller of Indiana State University recently created a program called Mindfulness-Based Eating Awareness Training, or MB-EAT, which uses meditation to teach people how to start eating smaller portions. The idea behind MB-EAT is that when people start tasting their food again, instead of just wolfing it down unconsciously, they become more aware of their actual appetite. Instead of getting tricked by their emotions, which often tell you to eat whether you're hungry or not, people who eat mindfully can teach themselves to eat only when they're truly hungry. As Dr. Kristeller tells Boston.com, "Our taste buds actually get tired rather quickly. The mindfulness can help people undo habits that have been there for decades."

Dr. Kristeller's MB-EAT program is really very simple: The next time you're hungry for a snack, put a handful of raisins in a bowl and then close your eyes. Put one into your mouth and, keeping your eyes closed, eat it taking the smallest bites possible. Then take another one and eat it the same way, really trying to focus on experiencing the incredible flavor and sensations created by each tiny bite of those raisins.

When you eat them slowly and mindfully—instead of quickly and distractedly, the way most people eat snacks—you'll be stunned by how much flavor each raisin has. You'll quickly realize that you can actually satisfy whatever hunger you were feeling with just a handful of them, as opposed to wolfing down a whole box.

Then try the same exercise with a cookie or ice cream (though as a vegan I would strongly recommend you try almond, soy, or rice milk, which is much better for you than milk-based ice creams but still tastes great!). As you eat it, really focus on experiencing just how rich and satisfying that single bite tastes. And then leave it at that. If you feel an urge to have more, don't give in to it and dig back into the container again and again until you're bloated and feeling like crap about yourself. Accept that you got all you needed out of that one bite.

That might sound impossible to people who've spent too many nights devouring tubs of rocky road and cookies and cream, but to someone who meditates, it actually sounds perfectly doable. Because once again, meditation trains your brain to see the distractions for what they are rather than be entangled in them.

Another way to help yourself to slow down and be mindful when you eat is to focus on where your food came from. Americans have developed a very bad habit of thinking that food originates in its packaging—that raisins are supposed to come in a box, or peaches in a can, or even that a cut of meat has always been wrapped in plastic, as opposed to once having been attached to an animal. And it's understandable—most of us weren't raised on farms, we were raised shopping in supermarkets. Our relationship with food is solely as consumers, not as producers.

But try to stop and take the time to really think about how that piece of fruit you're eating was made—how a seed had to be planted in the ground and then nurtured with water (and hopefully not exposed to any pesticides) and sunlight until it was ripe. How a laborer had to pick it without harming it, then haul it around until it was ready to be put in a truck and then brought to you. When you think about all the work and effort that went into the raisin or blueberry you're about to put into your mouth, you'll get much more enjoyment out of it. You'll have a much greater appreciation for what you're eating, and you won't feel the need to eat nearly as much as if you were just mindlessly chewing away while you watched TV or surfed the net.

Conversely, if you really thought about the origins of that ice cream you're about to dig into, you'd probably be a lot less likely to binge out and eat the whole thing in one sitting. If you thought about how each of those bites will contain ingredients like disodium phosphate, benzyl acetate, monostearate, propylene glycol, sodium benzoate, polysorbate 80, potassium sorbate, and modified cornstarch, then you'd be a lot more likely to stop after one small bowl, no matter how good it tasted.

That's the power of mindfulness—when you're conscious of

what you're actually putting into your body, as opposed to just giving yourself over to your cravings, you're going to eat much more selectively and healthily.

IT'S OKAY TO MESS UP

Meditation is going to make it much easier for you to be conscious of what you're eating, but perhaps just as important, it's also going to help you remember that it's not the end of the world if you do mess up and break your diet. A lot of folks tend to rely on "willpower" when it comes to dieting. In other words, they try to force themselves not to have what they think they want. They don't question whether or not the desire is real but try to refuse to give in to it.

The problem with that approach is that often when those people eventually break down and have that cookie or piece of cake (as we all do at some point), they feel that they've somehow lost that "power" they've been clinging to. And instead of getting back on their diet, they feel "powerless" to fight their urges and they start bingeing all over again.

Trust me, I've been there. Even though I've been a vegan for fifteen years, there have been dozens, if not hundreds, of times where I've slipped up and given in to an urge. Maybe it was snatching a forkful of fish off of a friend's plate and gobbling it down before they could even say "Stop!" Or even just allowing myself a little egg noodle.

The key is, when I do break down and "cheat" with a piece of fish, it doesn't rob me of my focus or dedication. I don't start telling myself, "I'm too weak to do this," or that now I'm no longer a vegan.

While my intention is to live a vegan lifestyle, I'm not perfect. And I accept my imperfection. Which is why when I slip up, I don't start worrying about what other vegans would "think" if they knew I'd eaten some meat. Because if I allow myself to get caught up in those distractions, then I'll feel like I've "failed" at being a vegan and will find myself back eating meat all the time again. Which of course in my eyes would be the *real* failure.

Instead, I consider what just happened—basically that I became distracted by an urge—and rather than beat myself up over it, I just return to my vegan practice the next time I sit down to a meal.

I also want to note that as we've already discussed, meditation dramatically cuts down on stress. This is very important as it relates to diet, because one of the things stress does is make you feel hungrier than you actually are. When you're stressed out, your brain basically starts sending out the same signals that it would if you were actually starving.

"Stress affects the same signals as famine does. It turns on the brain pathways that make us crave dense calories—we'll choose high fat, high sweet foods, or high salt," Elissa Epel, the founder and director of the Center for Obesity Assessment, Study, and Treatment at the University of California–San Francisco tells *Greater Good*, a journal of the University of California–Berkeley. "When we have a 'stress brain,' food is even more rewarding."

This connection between emotional stress and eating is even stronger among women. Epel says that surveys have shown 50 to 60 percent of women eat for emotional reasons rather than because of hunger. What that means is that when you move through life in a highly anxious and emotional state, it's likely that you're going to try to use food, especially sweets, to soothe that anxiety. But the truth is that the treats will never drown out the anxiety or uneasiness you might be feeling. All they're going to do is make you gain weight and most likely feel even worse about yourself.

Professor Kristeller also found that meditation was particularly helpful for women who were struggling with weight loss. Working with Duke University's world-famous Diet and Fitness Center, Professor Kristeller put a group of obese women through a four-month version of MB-EAT, with an emphasis on mindfulness. At the end of the course, she found that the women had already begun to develop healthier relationships with the food they were eating and as a result were losing weight. According to Professor Kristeller, "their success at losing weight was directly related to the degree to which they used mindfulness techniques."

As the iconic Buddhist monk Thich Nhat Hanh recently said in an interview with *Oprah* magazine, mindful eating is one of the most powerful stress relievers that we have at our disposal. "If I can look deeply into my food and take this time as a meditation—just as important as my sitting or walking meditation time—I receive the many gifts of the cosmos that I would not otherwise profit from if my mind were elsewhere. Because if I eat and am consumed by my worries and projects, I am eating a lot of stress and fear and this is harmful to my body and mind."

UN-COMFORTING FOOD

Understanding the link between stress and emotional eating is especially important for African-Americans, since, as we're constantly reminded, it's easy to perceive being African-American as particularly stressful. I've come to understand over time that you should never let outside influences affect your relationship with the world. Ultimately, you have complete control over whether you are happy or unhappy in life. But I also understand that whether it's being profiled by cops, consistently stereotyped by the media, or judged by potential employers, African-Americans are forced to deal with a lot of perceived stresses that are unique to our situation.

Unfortunately, one of the ways that we've collectively come to deal with those stresses is through eating so-called comfort foods. You know, foods like fried chicken, ribs, corn bread, mac 'n' cheese, and fried fish, which we tell each other will bring a sense of peace into our lives.

I was certainly raised that way. Growing up, it was almost as if eating "comfort food" was the most accessible way of dealing with the stresses, disappointments, and injustices that seemed to be inherent in the African-American experience. If you questioned your plate of ham hocks, black-eyed peas, and corn bread, it was almost like you were questioning your blackness.

But the sad truth is that any "comfort" those foods created only lasted for a moment. Because what happens just a few minutes after you polish off a plate of succulent ribs? Or put away a fat juicy steak? That's right, you catch the "itis." That's the term that black folks affectionately use to describe the sluggish feeling you get after eating soul food, but the truth is there's nothing cute about the "itis." Instead, that feeling of lethargy is your body's way of telling you that what you just ate wasn't good for you. And it's not a subtle warning either.

Yet people ignore that warning for years and years because they're simply not listening to what their bodies are telling them. How much more clear could your body be about the dangers of eating ribs than making you want to fall asleep moments after you've eaten them? Not much. But because they're distracted, people continue to ignore those warnings and pollute their bodies with harmful, unhealthy food until tragically, in many cases, it's too late.

So while soul food might be "comforting" to our emotions, it's not comforting to our bodies. Rather than bring you peace, these foods only end up making it more likely that you're going to have a serious health problem with high blood pressure, obesity, or strokes.

Trust me, when it came to soul food, I used to get down with the best of them. I've often said that back in the day I'd eat ribs, flanks, chittlins, buffalo wings, pig's feet . . . probably even an elephant's ass if you had put it on a plate in front of me. I never spent a moment considering what sort of damage that food was wreaking on me because I had grown up listening to the world instead of my body. And the world told me that greasy, fatty meats should make me happy and content. So that's what I believed, despite all the evidence to the contrary. Until I woke up.

I use the term "wake up" because I believe that eating meat actually represents unconscious behavior. We all know in our hearts that eating meat is wrong—bad for what it does to our bodies and terrible for the suffering it creates for the animals that are killed on our behalf. When the Bible spoke of giving man "dominion" over the animals, the intention wasn't to cosign an industrial farming industry that slaughters more than ten billion land animals in the United States each year alone. A farming industry that is one of the biggest contributors to global warming. I suspect the damage eating meat is causing is why Albert Einstein once said, "Nothing will benefit human health and increase the chances for survival of life on earth as much as the evolution to a vegetarian diet."

Yet often until we learn how to be still through a tool like meditation, we can't hear that truth in our hearts because we're so distracted by the noise of those who would have us believe eating meat is okay. I can say without reservation that I would have never become a vegan if I hadn't started meditating first. Without meditation, I would have continued to be a sheep. A follower who kept engaging in harmful acts because everyone else was doing it too. Meditation gave me both the clarity to see that I didn't like harming animals and then the confidence to actually act on that information. Once I woke up, I could see that passing out on the sofa after dinner isn't a good thing. That there must be a reason my body could barely function after I ate meat. Once I woke up, I could look at a rib and make that connection that it actually came from an animal that suffered very badly.

Thankfully I woke up before I could do any further damage to myself, or even worse, pass those habits along to my children. And hopefully after reading this section, if you still eat meat, you'll wake up too.

TIPS FOR MINDFUL EATING

I know that most of you weren't expecting a lecture on eating meat in a book about meditation, but one of the wonderful things about operating out of stillness is that it allows you to address issues in your life that you might not even have been aware of.

But ultimately, as much as I'd love for each and every one of you to cut meat out of your diet, the first step I'd like you to take is simply being a more mindful eater. The more you meditate, the more you'll naturally become more mindful, but I also want to share a few simple tips that you can incorporate into your lifestyle that will speed up your mindfulness:

- Turn off the TV when you eat. This is one of the most common forms of mindless eating. When you eat while you watch TV, you end up barely paying attention to your food. Which is why it becomes so easy to eat way more than you ever intended to without even realizing it.
- Unplug your computer too. Even a decade ago this probably wasn't an issue for most people, but today eating while surfing the net probably rivals TV as a cause of mindless eating.

- Don't eat while you drive. No matter how hungry you feel, you're not going to starve if you wait a few minutes to get where you're going and then eat. Even if you simply sit in your car with the ignition off and eat once you get there, it's a much more mindful experience than eating while you're driving. Plus it's safer too.

- Try eating in silence. I know that this seems to run counter to what many of us consider to be a desirable eating experience— good food *and* good conversation—but eating in silence really does promote mindfulness. Obviously you're not going to eat every meal in silence, but see if you can commit to at least one meal a week where instead of talking to someone, you pour all your focus and energy into the food you're putting into your body. A lot of people are starting to see the value in this. At the Google headquarters in Mountain View, California, the company hosts an hour-long wordless lunch once a month. "Interestingly enough, a lot of the participants are the engineers, which pleases us very much," Olivia Wu, an executive chef at Google, told *The New York Times*. "I think it quiets the mind. I think there is a real sense of feeling restored so that they can go back to the crazy pace that they came from."

- Eat slowly. With our schedules getting busier and our time seemingly stretched thinner and thinner, I know it gets tempting to rush through meals. Especially when so much food today is marketed to be eaten "on the go." But instead of wolfing down that sandwich or hamburger, try to eat it as slowly as you can. First, make sure you put your fork down after each bite. You might not even be aware of it, but you probably are already getting your next piece of food ready while you're still chewing your last bite. By simply remembering to put your fork back on your plate after you take a bite, you can dramatically slow down your pace. Then, after you do take a bite, whenever you feel like you normally would be ready to swallow, try to chew *another* fifteen times. It might feel awkward at first, but if you can condition yourself to chew your food longer and slower, it's going to go a long way toward creating a mindful eating experience.

And finally, try to remember that while eating mindfully might feel strange at first, it's actually the *most* healthy and rewarding relationship you can have with the food you eat. Which is why while the findings of the MB-EAT program and what they're doing at Google are really encouraging, the fact is people have been employing techniques like this for thousands and thousands of years. Even the Buddha himself was known to promote mindful eating as a path to contentment. "Hunger is the supreme disease," he taught, while also reminding people, "True happiness is the end of craving."

OUR COLLECTIVE HEALTH

Given that such highly respected institutions as Harvard, UCLA, Massachusetts General Hospital, the Mayo Clinic, and so many others are going on record with the fact that meditation improves our brains and promotes better health across the board, whenever I hear politicians complaining about our health care system, I wish they could understand how much suffering we could relieve and how much money we could save by promoting meditation.

Dr. Benson, who conducted the study on sleep and meditation at Harvard over thirty years ago, has a great analogy for the role meditation can play in our national health care debate. He says that medical treatment is like a three-legged stool: One leg is pharmaceuticals, one is surgery, and one is mind–body interactions like meditation and yoga. But as a society, we're only focused on those first two legs. Collectively, we need to start paying much more attention to that mind–body leg, or else that stool is going to break and we're all going to fall on our butts!

We don't have enough money for good schooling or housing in this country, yet we're spending hundreds of millions of dollars on poor people (and increasingly the middle class too) without insurance who have to go to emergency rooms to treat conditions like high blood pressure, asthma, hypertension, pneumonia, bad circulation, and migraines. We could be treating—and even better, helping people avoid—so many of those ailments by simply teaching them how to meditate. It would cost only a fraction of the money we spend on emergency room visits and would go so far to improve the health and happiness of our country.

On a personal level, I can't remember the last time I got a cold. That doesn't mean I won't get one tomorrow, but it does mean that since I've started meditating, my nervous system has grown much stronger. I'm constantly on planes, arriving in cities in the middle of the night, going in and out of hotels—the type of lifestyle that would typically leave a person run-down and sick all the time. But I've never felt healthier. And I attribute that to the effect meditating has had on my nervous system.

Doctors and scientists around the country are noticing the same thing too. In fact, last year a study in the *American Journal of Health Promotion* found that people who practiced TM for five years experienced a 28 percent cumulative decrease in physician fees during that time period. Considering that the average family of four pays around nineteen thousand dollars a year in health costs, that's a pretty big incentive to start the practice.

So to anyone out there who's worried about their weight, or worried about heart disease, or worried about their rising medical costs, I want to ask you this:

Is there any good reason why you wouldn't be interested in not only saving yourself thousands of dollars every year, but also potentially saving your *life,* by simply sitting in silence for twenty minutes two times a day?

I didn't think so.

PART FOUR

Living Up to Your Potential

CHAPTER 10

THE POWER OF THE PRESENT

Not long ago I was at a party talking to a famous fashion designer when the conversation turned to how I dealt with the stress of overseeing so many businesses, running several charities, having a personal life, and of course being a father. "Russell, I hear the way you stay sane is meditation," he said. "So tell me, what's the number one benefit you get from it?"

"Oh, that's easy," I said with a big smile. "It helps me stay awake during the day."

The second I said that, I could tell the guy was confused. Did I mean I have narcolepsy? That if it wasn't for meditation, I would be falling asleep at my desk and nodding off during meetings?

We got interrupted before I got a chance to explain myself that night, but now I want to clarify what I meant.

When I said I wanted to be awake during the day, I wasn't talking about being *physically* tired. If that were my problem, I could just drink coffee (which I rarely, if ever, do) or an energy drink. Or try some of the less legal forms of stimulation I used back in the day.

No, I was talking about being *present*.

You see, we're all physically awake during the day. Not so many of us, however, are present.

And presence is the source that everything positive, creative, happy, beautiful, and loving in your life is going to flow from.

When I speak of being present, I mean being truly connected to the moment. Where the distractions and noise of the world fade away and your mind is in the now. Instead of the past or the future.

I realize that when I use terms like "the moment" or "in the now," it might sound a little new agey to some of you. "Oh, Russell's going off on his Zen stuff right now," you might be thinking.

But there's really nothing at all exotic or mystical about being present. It's actually a state that we're all familiar with, that we all experience (hopefully) on a daily basis.

For example, at the very moment you laugh at a funny joke, that's being present. Becoming transfixed as you watch your favorite football team score a touchdown to win the game is being present too. As is getting so "into" a book that you almost forget to breathe.

We're all familiar with that sensation, even if we don't think of it as being "present." We all know what it's like to become so completely immersed in an activity that the distractions of life that usually seem so loud can barely be heard anymore. Because when you're watching your team score that touchdown, you're not thinking about the report you've got to hand in at work next week. Just as when you're turning those pages in a great thriller, you're not thinking about the bills you've got to pay. You're just enjoying the moment.

Take dancing. Why are some people great dancers and other people just can't seem to catch a beat? We like to joke that black folk are naturally funky and that white people don't know how to move, but of course that's all BS. I've seen plenty of white guys get all the way down on the dance floor, just as I've seen plenty of brothers who can't dance to save their lives.

What makes a great dancer isn't background or skin color, it's being present. When someone is really moving to a song, they're completely connected to the music. They're not worried about what other people in the club are thinking about them, they're just reacting to the notes of the music that they hear.

And if they're really plugged in, then they start moving *between* the notes. If you've ever watched a really great dancer, then you know what I'm talking about. Not only are they moving perfectly in sync with the bass line, the drums, and the guitars, but they also seem to be moving to notes in the spaces between those sounds. When Michael Jackson would do his signature kick, it wasn't to the beat. It was *between* the beats. That's how connected he was to the music. When he was dancing, he was completely present.

Now imagine if you could move through life being as connected as Michael Jackson was when he was dancing. Or as connected as you feel when you're laughing at an incredible comedian like Chris Rock.

It doesn't have to be something you only dream of doing. All of us possess that presence in our hearts. We all have the ability to be as present as MJ was when he was dancing, as Michael Jordan was when he was playing basketball, or as Chris Rock is when he's up onstage telling a joke.

We all have that inside of us, it's just that we're often too distracted by the noise of the world to realize it. But when the distractions of the world fade away, you can take those seconds of presence you feel laughing at a joke or hearing your favorite song and *extend* them. So that you don't just feel that way every once in a while but can actually move through life feeling connected and present.

To help you accept this truth, in this section I'm going to break down all the ways that meditation will help you become the best possible you and live up to your full potential as a human being.

But I also realize that many of you also probably came to these pages because you'd like to replicate some of the success I've had in the business world. So while I'll discuss the ways that meditation will make you more balanced and compassionate as well as less judgmental, I'll also highlight how those qualities will actually make you a better businessperson too.

CHAPTER 11

FINDING YOUR FOCUS

As you've already seen, there are a lot of reasons to meditate. But whenever I'm trying to give someone who's on the fence about meditation a very practical reason to do it, I usually tell them this: "Meditation is going to let you accomplish twice as much while only putting in half the effort."

Think about that.

Imagine if day in and day out you were able to be twice as productive as your coworkers. If every day you read twice as many reports as the guy in the cubicle next to you, taught twice as much material as the other teachers, or washed twice as many dishes as the other guys in your kitchen. How long would it be before you got promoted in that office, in that school, or in that restaurant? Not long at all. I can tell you that if someone in my office suddenly started doing twice as much work in half the normal time, I would notice that transformation.

And reward it too.

So if being more focused and productive is something that sounds attractive to you, then consider the studies that have proved people who meditate are able to hold their attention on tasks much longer than those who don't.

For instance, recently the University of California–Santa Barbara conducted a study on how meditation affects test-taking ability, which requires tremendous focus. In the study, a group of college students were asked to take the GRE (Graduate Record Examination). Then the students were split into two groups; one group took an intensive meditation class, the other an intensive class on nutrition.

After two weeks of class, each group was asked to take the GRE again. The group that studied nutrition didn't show any improvement, but the group that had meditated saw their average GRE verbal score go from 460 to 520. The meditation group also showed improvement on tests they were given on memory and focus.

If you've ever studied for the GRE or the SAT, then you know jumping up sixty points is a big deal. The kind of improvement that people often spend thousands of dollars on tutoring or classes to hopefully achieve.

Similarly, researchers from George Mason University and the University of Illinois recently conducted a study to find out if meditation could help college students increase their focus and retain more information from their lectures. The researchers found that students who meditated before their lecture scored better on a quiz that followed the lecture than those who didn't. "Data from this study suggest that meditation may help students who might have trouble paying attention or focusing," said one of the researchers, Professor Robert Youmans of George Mason.

Another study, entitled "Intensive Meditation Training Improves Perceptual Discrimination and Sustained Attention," was also recently published in *Psychological Science* and described similar findings. In this study, researchers tested two groups—one that had been taught meditation, one that hadn't—on their ability to focus on a task that required them to distinguish small differences between things they saw. Not surprisingly, the group that meditated scored much better on the tests. According to the researchers, this improvement in focus "persisted five months after the retreat, particularly for people who continued to meditate every day."

And it's not only scientists claiming that meditation improves your focus. Many business leaders have come to the same conclusion. *Business Insider* magazine recently included me in an article entitled "14 Executives Who Swear by Meditation," and in reading it I noticed that the two words all these business leaders kept mentioning were "focus" and "clarity." Robert Stiller, who founded Green Mountain Coffee, said, "If you have a meditation practice, you can be much more effective in a meeting. Meditation helps develop your abilities to focus better and to accomplish your tasks."

And Steve Rubin, who used to run United Fuels International, said

I really believe that in the not-so-distant future, we're going to see more and more companies making meditation part of their "official" corporate culture. Someone who's always out in front of the trends is my good friend Arianna Huffington, who recently started offering meditation classes to her employees at *The Huffington Post* and AOL. Why did she do it? "Stress reduction and mindfulness just don't make us happier and healthier, they're a proven competitive advantage for any business that wants one," she explained.

Well, most businesses (or at least the successful ones) are always looking for competitive advantages, so expect more CEOs to be following Arianna's lead (as they often do). . . .

that thanks to meditation, he has "the mental clarity and alertness for both laser-like focus on the details as well as broad comprehension."

Many of the executives also spoke of how meditation helped them make better decisions. Roger Berkowitz, the CEO of Legal Sea Foods, said, "Sometimes, I'm wrestling with an issue before meditation, and afterward the answer is suddenly clear." And Ramani Ayer, former chairman and CEO of the Hartford, a financial services company, noted, "Importantly, it has helped me to make clearer, more effective decisions on the job."

I've had a similar experience in my own career, where I've found that when I'm focused, I can look at a seemingly complex situation and instead of feeling overwhelmed by it, be able to see it clearly. Which in turn lets me make a decision that usually ends up being the right one. For example, I remember once RushCard didn't make any profit just one year after it made fifteen million in profit. The brand was just flat, but people tried to convince me that it had flat-*lined*. From my friends to my accountants to my senior executives, everyone was trying to convince me to pull the plug on the card. It was true that it had undergone a big shift, but I didn't let myself get distracted by all the anxiety I was hearing.

Instead, I took a very clear-eyed, unemotional look at the situation and decided that the company wasn't dead, it had just reached a stage where it needed to evolve. So while everyone was yelling for me to pull the plug, I actually put even *more* money into the company. Instead of tearing it apart, I reinvested in its core and gave it new life. And it worked. The next year, we were back to making a profit and all those naysayers tried to act like they had never called for me to abandon ship!

But without the focus and calmness that I've developed through meditation, I would have never been able to look past all that anxiety and see the potential the RushCard still had. As the Christian yogi Yogananda once wrote, "All successful men and women devote much time to deep concentration. They are able to dive deeply within their minds and to find the pearls of right solutions for the problems that confront them."

I also find it very telling that the only book Steve Jobs ever downloaded on his iPad was *Autobiography of a Yogi,* by Yogananda, the yogi I just quoted. In fact, in his bestselling biography of Jobs, Walter Isaacson wrote that *Autobiography of a Yogi* was "the guide to meditation and spirituality that he had first read as a teenager, then re-read in India and had read once a year ever since."

No entrepreneur ever did more with technology to bring people together than Steve Jobs, yet what book did he make a point of re-reading every year?

A book about stillness and meditation.

The beautiful thing about meditation is that when you're consistent with your practice, those "pearls" don't come to you just while you're meditating. Instead, as you practice, you'll find that they begin to appear over the course of your day. It can be very subtle too. You won't necessarily be sitting down and thinking very "hard" about whether to take a new job or commit to a certain relationship. Instead, you can just be driving in your car, or making dinner, and you will hear a soft voice telling you the answer to whatever question has been troubling you. It might say, "Yes, it's true that job will pay you more, but you don't feel good about that company. You don't like the product and the guy who would be your boss made you feel uncomfortable. Say no." And when you hear that voice, you'll know that you've found your pearl. Even though the thought of turning it down might have made you anxious—"Suppose I never get offered a job that pays this much again? What if I say no and then get fired from my current job in six months?"—that calm, focused voice that said no spoke with more authority than the anxiety. That's how you know that saying no is the right decision.

As Yogananda said, being able to access deep concentration and focus has always been a skill of successful people, but it's become even more of a necessity in the Internet age. Don't get me wrong, I love so many things about the Internet and social media. In many ways, the strengths of the Internet, and of new technology, are similar to some of the strengths of meditation—they help bring people together and remind us of all the things we share in common. The main reason I run a website called GlobalGrind.com is that I firmly believe that the Internet will help young people overcome the cultural barriers that have held back previous generations.

There can be a healthy relationship between the stillness inside of us and the technology that can connect us with others, but only if we really work on cultivating that stillness. Otherwise, the technology is so omnipresent that it will drown out that stillness and focus.

While it's amazing that you can get on Twitter and find out about a mass demonstration in Egypt as it's happening, it can also be extremely distracting to keep looking at pictures of what your friends just ate or read about what just happened on a reality show. A lot of the information we get on social media is nothing but noise, a constant buzz that just dilutes our focus.

And if I'm being honest, I'm guilty of this myself. Even though I definitely feel that many of my tweets and the messages I post to Facebook contain information that's going to help bring people together, I put a lot of noise out there too.

The problem is listening to that noise can become very addictive. How many times have you been working on an idea and just when you come to a difficult point, you suddenly get an urge to check your e-mail, or log on to Facebook? Instead of maintaining your focus and working through whatever problem you've encountered, you give yourself over to the welcome diversion of your cell phone.

I see this in social situations all the time too. Have you ever looked around a party and thought it seemed like half the people were staring at their cell phones? Or even standing on the dance floor and looking at their phones? You know they're not really responding to an urgent e-mail. Instead, like most of us can, they're feeling a little shy or awkward in a social environment. Yet instead of getting past that awkwardness and walking over, introducing themselves to a stranger and starting up a conversation, or even just dancing by themselves, they're taking refuge in the distraction their cell phones provide.

But getting past that awkwardness and shyness and striking up a conversation with a stranger is often how you take your life to the next level. Striking up a conversation with someone you barely know might be how you meet the man who will become your husband or the person who wants to invest in your business. Or simply make a new friend.

You don't make those types of connections when you're staring at your phone in the middle of a party. But you can make them when you feel at ease with yourself enough to take a chance and introduce yourself to a stranger. That's the type of ease and confidence that meditation promotes.

CHAPTER 12

THE HEAVINESS OF
SUCCESS AND FAILURE

Being more focused isn't the only way meditation is going to help you in your career. On a philosophical level, it's going to allow you to get past the misconception that trips up so many of us: that our lives are defined by our "successes" and "failures."

If you follow me on Facebook or Twitter, then you already know that one of my favorite quotes from the Hindu holy book the Bhagavad Gita is "You have control over your work alone, never the fruit."

There are a lot of different ways you could interpret that passage, but to me it's always meant "Stop worrying about how much money you make off your work (the fruit) and instead just stay focused on your work itself." Because when you embrace the process of your work, instead of focusing on the results, you'll always be happier, plus do a much better job.

Of course, that's easier said than done in a culture that puts so much emphasis on success (the "fruit") and failure (the absence of "fruit") but not nearly enough on the actual process of making that fruit.

This is where meditation can be extremely helpful. When you take those twenty minutes and allow yourself to calm down and shut out the distractions, you'll find that it becomes easier to see that your true happiness lies in the process, not the results.

When I meditate, I can see that what makes me happy isn't getting a fat check or buying a new toy, but coming up with creative ways I can help other people realize their dreams. That might seem a bit corny, but it's true. And it's always been that way for me. I got into hip-hop because I wanted to help other people experience the joy I felt the first time I heard someone rap. I wanted to help rappers reach new audiences and I wanted people who might not otherwise hear about it to come to the music.

My career in music was always about helping other people share their gift. When I was working with Run-DMC or LL Cool J or Public Enemy, I woke up every morning focused on how I could help them reach more people and share more of their gift.

If I've ever stumbled in my career, it's only been in those moments where I've lost sight of this truth and become more focused on the results. When I've become more focused on what a company is worth than whether or not I actually enjoy working on it.

Meditating helps remind me every day to re-embrace the

process. So if I love working on new designs for a fashion label, getting the opportunity to do that will be enough for me. Whether those clothes are flying off the shelves or barely moving, I'm going to be okay. Because I know if I stay focused on the process of making the clothes that I love, eventually other people are going to pick up on that passion and embrace it.

Meditation also helps you get past the anxiety that always accompanies "wins" and "losses." People don't like to hear this, but the truth is that "losses" and "failure" are actually very important parts of the process of becoming good at whatever it is you do.

To use Steve Jobs as an example again, today we think of him as one of the greatest success stories of all time, as the man who made Apple one of the most admired brands in the world. And while there's no doubt he deserves that legacy, he wasn't always viewed as a success. Yes, he experienced tremendous success after he initially helped start Apple, but he also very publicly got booted out of the company a few years later. After that, in the eyes of the tech world, he was a "failure," a guy who had a shot and blew it.

That sense of having "failed" would have discouraged a lot of people, but Steve never gave up on the process—in his case a love of inventing new ways to communicate—and eventually was able to make everyone forget his previous "failure."

In a famous speech he gave at Stanford University in 2005, Steve said that in many ways "failing" publicly was actually a blessing. "It turned out that getting fired from Apple was the best thing that

Steve Jobs will be remembered, rightfully, as one of the great innovators of his generation. But we shouldn't forget that so much of his philosophy and approach was rooted in the ancient practice of meditation. This is what he told his biographer Walter Isaacson: "If you just sit and observe, you will see how restless your mind is. If you try to calm it, it only makes it worse, but over time it does calm, and when it does, there's room to hear more subtle things—that's when your intuition starts to blossom and you start to see things more clearly and be in the present more. Your mind just slows down, and you see a tremendous expanse in the moment. You see so much more than you could see before. It's a discipline; you have to practice it."

could have ever happened to me," he said. "The heaviness of being successful was replaced by the lightness of being a beginner again. . . . It freed me to enter one of the most creative periods of my life."

And if you think about Steve's legacy, most of the things he's remembered for today—the iPod, iPhone, and iPad—all were created *after* he'd been labeled a failure.

I believe meditation helped him stay focused on the process and helped him throw off not only the heaviness of being successful but the heaviness he must have also felt after being called a failure. Because at its root, that heaviness is just a big ball of anxiety.

I've felt the weight of that heaviness too. Looking back, I used to overthink *everything* when it came to my businesses. Publicly, I played the role of someone who didn't have a care in the world—it was all about partying and having fun. But inside, forget about it. I was a mess. Every business decision I was involved in would become gut-wrenching.

I still remember how I was absolutely consumed with doubt when I was first approached about selling Def Jam Recordings. I was being offered forty million dollars—a tremendous amount of money but all I could see was fear. Day and night, I was tormented. Should I sell the company? Was it for the right price? If I waited a few more weeks, could I get a better price? Was I about to get ripped off? And once I did sell, what would I do next? It was like those questions were playing on a twenty-four-hour-a-day loop in my mind. I could have been sitting in a club surrounded by models—which for a lot of people is the very picture of having "made it"—but emotionally I was probably the most miserable person in the room.

In the end, I decided not to sell, even though everyone around me thought I was insane for turning down so much money. My initial reaction to the offer was that it just wasn't the right time, and despite all the torment I put myself through, it turned out my first reaction was my best one. As is almost always the case. Because just eighteen months later I got an offer for $112 million, which I did accept.

And it wasn't just big decisions, like whether or not to sell a company. Getting hung up about failure used to get me bent out of shape all the time back then and distract me from being focused on the process. I can remember in the mid-1980s I produced a record with an R & B group I loved called Blue Magic. They weren't young and hip like Run-DMC or Public Enemy, but their music was so beautiful that I was convinced it would set the world on fire. When it came out, the album received great reviews but "only" got played on the old-school stations. To me, that was a great failure. I made a brand-new record and already it was being seen as "old school"? I felt dispirited, like the record had been rejected.

When that happened, I should have appreciated that I had been able to put my resources toward helping something that was beautiful and reflected what was in my heart.

But instead of doing that, I started feeling sorry for myself. For the first time in my career, I had promoted something that I was sure the rest of the world was going to share my passion for, but they didn't. The heaviness of that perceived failure basically stopped me from ever getting back into the studio with Blue Magic and helping them share their beauty with the world.

Today, thanks to meditation, I don't get anxious about whether or not the world shares my vision right away or not. Just as I've stopped tearing myself apart over whether there's a right or wrong answer for every situation and learned to accept that inevitable ups and downs are a necessary part of my journey.

If holding on to a company feels like the right thing to do, then

SUCCESS THROUGH STILLNESS

I don't know of many people who've done a better job at keeping an even keel over the years than Oprah. No matter what's going on around her or what's being said about her, Oprah's managed to keep a laserlike focus on her vision.

So I'm not surprised at all that after meditating for the first time several years ago, Oprah had this to say: "I walked away feeling fuller than when I'd come in. Full of hope, a sense of contentment and deep joy. Knowing for sure that even in the daily craziness that bombards us from every direction, there is still the constancy of stillness. Only from that space can you create your best work and your best life."

I'm going to sell. If making records is what I feel passionate about, then I'm going to make them whether the world immediately reacts positively to them or not.

Before, I was on a roller coaster. If my stock was "up," I was riding high, but if it was "low" I was down in the dumps. Now I'm approaching my work from a much calmer perspective. So whether that stock goes up or it goes down, my heart rate stays the same.

I won't lie; that calmness can be disconcerting to my business partners. They're used to seeing people in my position go celebrate like crazy when a project makes money and get very angry and upset when it doesn't. But if I believe in an idea, I'm going to stick with it whether it brings back an investment at first or not. There have been many years when my business has operated in a deficit, but if the work is satisfying, then I'm excited.

My accountant actually took me aside the other day and told me in a very serious tone, "Russell, if you keep putting your money into all these ventures, you'll be broke in a few years."

I know that was supposed to be a sobering, maybe even scary, message, but any anxiety it might have created was only fleeting.

Because as soon as that anxiety moved out of my mind, I remembered I'm spending my money on light, fun things. On building yoga studios. On spreading hip-hop culture. On promoting artistic expressions through my TV and film companies. On promoting ethnic understanding. How could I ever stay anxious about that? If doing those things makes me go broke, then when that moment comes I'll just figure out a way to make some more money. Or maybe I won't. Maybe I'll just go to India and learn how to teach yoga. If I get to that moment, I'll deal with it. But I've conditioned my mind not to get entangled in worry, even if that's what my accountant might prefer!

Adopting this calm approach is why I encourage all my employees to practice meditation. One person who's taken to it right away and has really reaped the benefits is my COO Osman Eralp. When he first started working with me, Osman was so anxiety prone. No matter what issue was in front of us, he was worried about it—from whether a product was worth a multi-million-dollar investment to what color to paint the walls, Osman was always worked up.

But now that Osman is meditating every day, he's calmed down a lot. Instead of getting tripped up by every scenario that passes through his mind, he's allowing his thoughts to settle before he tries to act on them.

This is an especially important skill for someone like Osman, whose true gift is his creativity. When you are creative and full of imagination, *so* many ideas are going to come into your head. And to be blunt, while some of them are going to be genius, many more will be trash. The question is, how do you stop reacting to all that trash and learn how to zero in on the ideas that have real value?

The answer, of course, is meditation. Which is why I encourage all my employees to spend some time in stillness each day. Think about it: Do I want an organization filled with people who stay on that emotional roller coaster, quick to break out the champagne the moment something "hits" but equally quick to panic the moment they think something isn't working? Or do I want to be surrounded by people who are steady and thoughtful in their approach and take satisfaction simply from trying to do a good job? For me, it's an easy choice.

Another entrepreneur who encourages his employees to meditate for this very reason is someone I mentioned earlier, Ray Dalio, the founder of one of the largest hedge funds in the world. A lot of Ray's business philosophy revolves around his employees' being able to have very open conversations about issues they're facing without worrying about whether they're "right" or "wrong." Ray believes, and I agree with him, that's it's much more valuable for people to have a real exchange of information and ideas than to be surrounded by yes-men who are afraid to say what they think. Or even worse, will only say what they think you *want* them to say.

In an interview with Academy of Achievement, Ray said he values having meditators around him because the practice "promotes the ability to disagree without being trapped by emotion. To be able to talk about strength and weakness. To separate yourself from your weakness and look at it objectively is a very powerful thing."

Ray adds that while hundreds of people in his office meditate, not all of them do. But he says, "You can tell a big difference between someone who didn't meditate and someone who started." And just like I saw with Osman, what Ray notices is how much more powerful those people are after they learn how to stop operating out of an anxious space. Instead of always freaking out or being anxious about getting something wrong, Ray sees they "have open, thoughtful conversation, to find what the true answers are." And as Ray points out, that calmness isn't just good for business: "That clarity is going to be the biggest thing that can help mankind."

CHAPTER 13

FINDING CALM AND BALANCE

've been talking about how meditation can help you let go of the anxiety you might feel at your work or in your career, but it's important to understand that that sense of calm and being balanced will extend to all aspects of your life.

Many people who practice meditation, especially those who consider themselves Buddhists, refer to achieving this balance as being in a state of "equanimity." If you're not familiar with it, equanimity is defined as "evenness of mind, especially under stress."

Now, I'll be honest, I didn't know what that word meant before I started hanging out with some Buddhists. I have, however, been aware of the state they're describing for a long time. What they call "equanimity," I've always called "cool." And at their essence, they really mean the same thing.

Back when I was a kid, the coolest guys were movie stars like

If you've ever read *The Color Purple,* then I don't have to tell you what a wonderful writer Alice Walker is. And in an article for *The New York Times,* she credited much of her success as a writer to the balance meditation brought into her life: "Meditation has been a loyal friend to me. It has helped me write my books. I could not have written *Possessing the Secret of Joy* without it; writing *The Temple of My Familiar* would have been impossible. *The Color Purple* owes much of its humor and playfulness to the equanimity of my mind as I committed myself to a routine, daily practice."

Richard Roundtree from *Shaft* or Ron O'Neal from *Super Fly.* For kids today, it would probably be Jay Z, who has that same sort of coolness, the same sense of being balanced no matter what is happening around him. Jay might be the coolest person I've ever met, and not just because he's sold millions of records and is married to Beyoncé (though it sure doesn't hurt). If you spent five minutes around Jay, you would see that he'd be cool with or without all that worldly success.

I believe what makes Jay so unflappable is that he's able to live in the moment. In the recording studio, in the streets, in a boardroom, onstage, wherever he's at. People might be going crazy around him, snapping pictures, slapping his back, or screaming his name, but you can sense that Jay never gets caught up in it. He's always connected to, and content with, what's happening in his own head.

And at his heart, Jay is a meditator. In his classic song "Can I Live," which is about dealing with the "valleys and peaks [and] expectations" of both hustling in the streets and being a rapper, Jay actually says his turning point came when he "stepped it up another level, meditated like a Buddhist."

The beautiful thing about meditation is that it allows you to access that cool guy (or girl) inside of you that's waiting to come out. The Jay Z–level cool that you know you possess but always seems just out of your reach.

You might not be married to Beyoncé or sell a million records, but when you meditate, you'll be able to access that part of you that people like to be around. The part of you that feels upbeat about things. That feels like you're moving toward your goals without frustration and anxiety. You'll be that cool guy who has it together and is able to come up with a plan when everyone else is running around like a chicken with its head cut off. Or that cool girl everyone looks up to, who everyone wants to be like, who is able to bring out the best in other people.

All you have to do to be that person is to let go of the anxiety that's built up in your mind. I know that the idea of letting go of your worries might sound very difficult, but meditation makes it possible.

Meditation is not going to get rid of whatever is making you anxious. If you're worried about your marriage, meditation is not going to magically fix your relationship. If you're worried about your job, meditation is not going to get you promoted. And as much as I wish it would, meditation is not going to bring back a loved one who passed away.

What meditation will do, however, is teach you how not to get stuck worrying about your marriage, your job, or even losing someone close to you, as difficult as that may sound. When you meditate, you'll learn how to let your thoughts exist on their own without getting too involved in them.

This is especially important when you encounter negative thoughts, which most of us do every day. Sometimes, it might even seem, *most* of the day. According to Dr. Philippe Goldin, who runs the Clinically Applied Affective Neuroscience laboratory at Stanford, meditation can change how you deal with those negative thoughts. In studies, Dr. Philippe has found that people's most common reaction to negative thoughts is to either push them away or obsess over them.

We've all felt that way at times. If something bad seems to happen, we either don't think about it at all or spend too much time thinking about it. We either walk around in denial or walk around like there's a black cloud hovering over our head. But neither of those approaches really works. Whether we try to ignore a problem or obsess over it, the result is always the same: That anxiety only gets louder.

What meditation provides is an alternate way to deal with anxiety. Meditation allows you to acknowledge what is happening in your life (instead of denying it) but then keep it moving (as opposed to obsessing over it). This is the healthiest way to move through life. As Dr. Goldin puts it, "The goal of meditation is not to get rid of thoughts or emotions. The goal is to become more aware of your thoughts and emotions and learn how to move through them without getting stuck."

Keep in mind, this applies to not only how you deal with anxious or negative situations but how you deal with positive ones too. Trust me, I've seen just as many people get stuck "celebrating" as I've seen get stuck worrying. In particular, I'd see this happen to a lot of the rappers I've worked with. They'd sign a new deal, or be given a gold record, and then want to run out and celebrate by buying a new car or dropping thousands of dollars in the club making it rain on a stripper. But after they'd drive that car around for a couple of days, or when they woke up the next morning after spending 10K in the club, they'd feel very empty inside.

Quite a few guys would confess this to me in almost apologetic terms, as if they'd messed up. "Russell, I don't know what's wrong with me," they'd say. "I went out and bought me and my boys all sorts of things after I signed my deal. And then we went and shut down the club. But even after all of that, I'm just not happy."

What I've always tried to explain to those artists is that the reason they're feeling out of whack is because they got too caught up in the celebrating. If you're an artist, what truly makes you happy isn't buying new cars or popping bottles. It's making beautiful music for other people to enjoy. That's it. You're going to be your happiest when you're in the studio writing a song, not when you're out celebrating how many records that song eventually sold.

So whether the emotion is a happy or sad one, in order to achieve a state of equanimity, you need to stay focused on not getting stuck on it. I'm not suggesting that you need to turn into Mr. Spock and be completely devoid of emotion. (I guess I'm showing my age.) But the more you learn how to use meditation to engage your emotions and then let them go, the less anxious and more free you'll feel.

In some ways I've been fortunate when it comes to anxiety. Maybe it's the way I'm wired, maybe it was the example of my parents—I can't really call it—but I've never really suffered from carrying a lot of worry around with me. Yes, as I mentioned, I tended to overthink business deals, but overall I generally had an upbeat outlook.

But as I've grown older, there have been situations that could have created a lot of anxiety for me. I lost both my parents, both of whom I was very close to. I got divorced. I watched my brother suffer through depression. I've lost vast amounts of money. I've had companies fail. I've been labeled out of touch and even, most recently, an Uncle Tom.

I've spent years and millions of dollars working on social initiatives like school reform, prison reform, drug law reform, anti-homophobia, and anti-Islamophobia. Issues that all directly affect the African-American community very deeply.

But when my new Internet network, ADD, released an admittedly poorly conceived parody about Harriet Tubman, I rightfully got taken to task on the Internet. Even though I apologized and explained that I was deeply sorry for not being sensitive to the underlying implications of the video, people really let me have it.

It was very difficult for me to know that I had offended, hurt, and disappointed so many people. Because of this, it could have been very easy to get wrapped up in anxiety and pull the plug on my network before it ever really got started. But I didn't.

And I credit that to meditation. If I hadn't found meditation, the worry would have eventually knocked me off balance. Maybe it would have been my divorce. Maybe it would have been the Harriet Tubman video. Maybe it would have been losing one of my parents. Or maybe it would have been getting caught up celebrating a so-called success. But thanks to meditation I've been able to maintain that balance.

A final example: When Barack Obama first ran for president, I worked extremely hard for him. I donated money, traveled the country going to every place that would have me, made phone calls, and did everything I could to make sure the hip-hop community was going to come out and vote.

I still vividly remember going to a party for his supporters on election night. After it became apparent he was really going to win, everyone around me started going crazy! People were doing double shots of tequila, dancing on tables, hugging each other and crying.

But as soon as the election was officially called, I was ready to go home. Not because I wasn't happy Obama won—I was—but because it's hard for me to get too excited about any kind of work that I do. Yes, I put in a tremendous amount of work for President Obama, but it's not like if Senator McCain had won I would have fallen to the floor in a heap sobbing. No, if McCain had won, you can believe the very next morning I would have rolled up my sleeves and gone to work trying to figure out a way to change his thinking on the issues that we disagreed on. In fact, I had even started working on a letter to him about several of those issues just in case he did win.

Some people might see that approach as cold or opportunist, but it's not. It's simply about not becoming stuck on any one emotion. If you become very happy when you win, then it stands to reason that you're going to get very sad when you lose. And in life, both wins and losses are inevitable. The key is to treat them the same. And meditation conditions you to do that.

Sometimes, when people see me about to leave a party "early" or turn down a round of shots when everyone else is getting turnt up, they'll say, "Russell, don't you miss out on celebrating? Don't you want to enjoy life?"

I have to tell them, I don't feel like I'm missing out on *anything*. Because a constant contentment is what I'm looking for. I'm more interested in feeling balanced and peaceful *all* of the time, not just when something "good" is happening. That sense of equanimity I find in meditation is what makes me truly happy.

Some friends have even asked me, "If you get less emotional about situations when you meditate, does that make you feel less alive?" And my answer is always a resounding "No!"

Today, sitting here well into middle age, I can say I'm truly a happy person, which is a beautiful thing to be able to say. Am I eternally blissful? No. But do I find moments when I'm ecstatic about being alive? Yes! And the more I meditate, the more I have those moments.

I'm talking about moments after I meditate where I feel *extra* alive. I even have some sessions that leave me feeling so blissful that they produce tears of joy. Forget about a morning coffee—can you imagine how alive you feel when you start off your day crying tears of joy? It really is an amazing experience.

And it's an experience that you can access too through meditation. Remember, *you* always control how you react to your thoughts. Not the other way around. Don't ever forget that *you* always have the ability to make a change in how you perceive and react to the world. That power is always within your grasp. You just have to learn how to harness it.

CHAPTER 14

CULTIVATING CREATIVITY

The older we get, the more we tend to undervalue creativity. It's as if creativity was a luxury we could afford when we were kids, but now that we're dealing with "adult issues," there's no time to play in fantasyland.

Of course just the opposite is true. The older we get, the more critical people become when we tap into our inherent creativity. Because that creativity is where all our good ideas come from.

Look at it like this: Pretend that you're a farmer trying to pick between two fields to plant your new crop in. One field is filled with rocks, thorn bushes, old branches, rabbit holes, all sorts of junk that is going to make your work very difficult. The other field has nothing but smooth, unspoiled soil.

Which one are you going to plant your crops in? The second one, right?

Well, your mind is the same as those fields. If it's filled with a lot of junk, it's going to be very hard to plant a successful crop there. And even if something good does grow in there, it's going to be very difficult for you to find it.

But when you can slow down and be still, your mind will be like the smooth soil of that second field. If properly cared for, it's going to be extremely fertile. As I wrote in *Super Rich,* "Stillness is the soil in which imagination is nourished, and our ideas can grow to incredible heights. The soil that can yield a crop that will sustain us for a lifetime."

In short, a calm mind is a creative mind. And a creative mind is going to bring a lot of success into your life.

I'll give you an example. In my many years in the entertainment industry, I've been around some amazing artists, in particular some of the greatest rappers of all time. Now, rapping might not be an art form that people associate with calmness and stillness, but I can tell you that from LL Cool J to Chuck D to Biggie Smalls to Jay Z, one trait that all those great artists share is an ability to operate out of stillness. There are a lot of rappers who worked as hard as those guys, but very few were able to dip into that well of creativity like they were.

When it was time to get on the mic and spit a verse, those guys were able to shut out all the distractions and delve inside. If you've never been inside a recording studio, trust me, there can be a *ton* of distractions. As a rule, rappers (and rock stars) like to be around a lot of people when they work, so it's not uncommon to have producers, engineers, managers, friends, groupies, journalists, maybe even a

Rick Rubin is not only one of the greatest producers alive, he's also one of my greatest friends. We founded Def Jam Recordings together and shared so many wonderful moments helping bring hip-hop to the world. One of Rick's greatest gifts is that he has an incredible ear—he simply can hear beauty and potential where others can't.

The first time we heard a demo tape from Public Enemy, truthfully I didn't think much of it. "Ah, sounds like some black punk rock stuff," I said. But right away Rick told me, "Russell, this is incredible, we have to sign them." And of course Rick was right.

And his ear hasn't been limited to hip-hop. From Johnny Cash to Slayer to the Red Hot Chili Peppers, Rich has been able to coax beautiful music from such a diverse group of artists. And I truly believe one of the main reasons he can connect with so many artists' voices as a producer is that he meditates.

He's actually been doing it since he was a little kid, when his pediatrician recommended it to him. There are times when he moves away from the practice, but he always comes back to it.

Toward the end of writing this book, I sent Rick an e-mail asking him for his thoughts on meditation and how it's helped him. The very same day, I received this response from him: "In meditation we experience the silence from which all creativity springs. The act of creation—whether from a blank page to a poem, an empty space to a building, a thought to a song or film—starts with a void. The more intimate a relationship we can build with that silent void, the more clearly the art can shine through and spring forth. Meditation is the vehicle to connect to that silence."

—Rick Rubin, Malibu 2013

few drug dealers all packed into the studio. It's a scene where it's easy for a rapper to become focused on everything *but* the music.

The great ones, however, never get lost in those distractions. Biggie in particular was legendary for his ability to stay focused. There could be all sorts of things going on—drinks being passed, blunts being rolled, people trying to holler at him about various projects—but he'd just sit in a chair with his eyes closed, seemingly oblivious to all the chaos around him. That was his way of connecting to the stillness inside of him, so that when it was time to get behind the microphone, he wasn't caught up in worrying about how his last record did or how this one might be received once it was released. No, when it was time to make a song, he was always able to connect with both the music he was hearing in his headphones and the poetry that was filling up his heart. The same way today artists like Jay Z or Lil Wayne are able to create entire songs without ever putting a word down on paper. Through being able to connect completely with the music, they are able to operate from that "zone" that the great ones are able to access.

That might not sound like a big deal, but I've seen so many artists get sidetracked by those distractions. And when it's time for them to get in the recording booth and execute their craft, their mind is somewhere else. Sure, they're rapping along to the beat, but they're not *connected* to it.

For example, I'm nowhere near as creative as Biggie was, or any of the rappers I just mentioned, but I do know this: When I was producing Run-DMC's classic hits like "Rock Box" and "Jam Master Jay," I felt completely still. I might not have used the term back then but it describes the state I was in.

I often tell the story of lying on the floor of a recording studio in downtown Manhattan and listening to the final mix of "Rock Box." I remember it being as if the entire world had stopped and the music was playing in slow motion. I could hear every subtle detail in that song, and the melody felt like it was alive. I was completely connected with what was coming through the speakers. It was magical.

I wasn't thinking about anything that had led up to that moment and I didn't have any thoughts of what might happen after the group had released it. All I could hear was that beat, that guitar riff, and Run-DMC's powerful vocals. I knew exactly what needed to be fixed and what shouldn't be touched. Outside of the birth of my children, I don't think I've ever been so happy, so completely engaged in the moment.

They might seem very different on the surface, but there's actually a strong connection between rapping and meditation. As I mentioned, Jay Z has talked about meditating in his rhymes, as have Lil Wayne, T.I., and RZA.

Several years ago I was interviewed for *Yoga Journal* with RZA and the Shaolin monk Shi Yan Ming, who said he considered what the Wu Tang Clan did on the mic to be actual meditation. "When people dance and listen to hip-hop, they are happy. This is also meditation. RZA, when he writes songs, uses philosophy to help people. He is giving people meditation," explained Master Ming.

Now, here's the thing: Most people assume that they can't control when those sorts of creative moments happen. Even when they do get a good idea, they'll say something like, "It just popped into my head," as if it was some sort of accident or lucky break.

But there's nothing accidental or lucky about accessing the good ideas you have inside of you. Remember, those ideas are already there, you've just had trouble finding them because all the junk in your mind has been obscuring them. Meditation will help you clean out that junk and find those good ideas.

How? Think of your mind as like one of those snow globes you used to play with as a kid. When you'd shake them up, the snow would be everywhere and it would kind of obscure what was inside the globe. But when you just let the globe be still, eventually all the snow would settle down to the bottom and you could clearly see what was inside it.

When you use meditation to allow your mind to be still, it's the same thing. Eventually all the distractions are going to settle down and you'll be able to see clearly what's inside of you.

I was recently at an event for the David Lynch Foundation (yes, they have a lot!) and I heard the comedian Russell Brand say that he thinks meditation will help him get rich (or in his case, richer). He said, "I literally had an idea drop into my brain while I was meditating which I think is worth millions of dollars."

I know exactly what Russell was talking about. I feel as though almost every time I meditate I'm able to access a great idea for my TV and film companies, or my new music label. Instead of being distracted, I am able to look at ideas through a clear prism and be extremely focused. In fact, the very idea of launching a TV and movie company came to me during meditation. And I'm sure that everyone who meditates has had a similar experience. Maybe not an idea worth millions of dollars, but certainly ideas that have real value, whether they're monetized or not.

And just as your sense of being focused isn't limited to the twenty minutes you're in actual meditation, it's the same with creativity. Russell's idea might have come to him while he was sitting in silence, but I'm sure he'd say that he feels more creative during his entire day since he started meditating.

I certainly do. And I'm far from alone. There are so many incredible

> "I went through two schools of acting, but I learned more about acting from meditating and my martial arts teacher."
> —Forest Whitaker

actors, musicians, directors, and comedians out there who all credit meditation with keeping their creative juices flowing. Judd Apatow. Sheryl Crow. Clint Eastwood. Jeff Garlin. Jeff Goldblum. India.Arie. Hugh Jackman. Lenny Kravitz. George Lucas. David Lynch. Madonna. Paul McCartney. Eva Mendes. Rosie O'Donnell. Gwyneth Paltrow. Martin Scorsese. Jerry Seinfeld. Howard Stern. Forest Whitaker.

These people all come from different backgrounds and create a diverse array of art. But meditation is a thread that ties them all together. That helps them hear that new song in their head, see the scene they want to film, or hear the joke they want to tell.

You can tap into the same sort of creativity that Jerry Seinfeld feels when he comes up with a new joke, Lenny Kravitz feels when he writes a song, or Forest Whitaker feels when he films a scene.

All it takes is sitting in silence.

CHAPTER 15

GETTING UNSTUCK

One of the most unfortunate misconceptions people have about their lives is that they're stuck in a certain situation. Whether it's a job, a relationship, a "mood," or even a physical location, they feel as if there's nothing they can do to change it.

But the fact is, no matter where you're from or what you've done, you're never stuck in *anything* unless you say you are.

And meditation will help you see this. Meditation will help you lift your foot up out of the emotional quicksand you thought was pulling you down and let you start walking freely again.

This is because when you sit in silence for twenty minutes twice a day, you will begin to realize that parts of your life that you thought were unmovable, unfixable, or uncomfortable are in fact none of those things. They only have the power you assign them.

When you let the noise distract you, it becomes very easy to move through life thinking, "Well, that's just the way I am." Or, "Hey, I'm not perfect. But nobody is. So people need to get off my back."

But when you sit there in silence each day, it becomes harder and harder to ignore those parts of your environment that you don't like. Or make you uncomfortable. To the point where you'll realize that it's actually easier to change those parts of your life than it is to keep on perpetuating a negative cycle.

So many of us, if we're being honest, get caught in these cycles. Where we do the same dumb shit over and over again. Even though it never makes us happy. I've certainly felt trapped in many of them.

I never really truly liked getting high, but there would be so many times where it would be four A.M. and I'd find myself smoking a woolly blunt (that's weed mixed with cocaine). I'd stagger home at ten A.M. and wake up the next afternoon feeling terrible about what I'd done and vowing to clean up my life. But two nights later, there I'd be at four A.M. again, holding another blunt or sniffing another line.

I used to find myself in the same sort of negative cycle with women. I'd chase them very hard but often run away just as hard after I'd caught them.

That was a very selfish attitude to have, and I hated that I used to make another person feel bad about herself simply because I couldn't control my desires.

Today while I'm still not so great when I'm single, but I'm much less selfish in my relationships. If I'm going to be 100 percent real, however, out of all the cycles I've found myself stuck in over the years, chasing women has been the hardest for me to break out of. I take a little solace in knowing it's said Lord Buddha's last problem was the flesh. I'm not free from neediness at all. But I have faith in the path that meditation has put me on. I have faith that even if I trip up from time to time, I can still get back on that right path. I don't feel like I'm *trapped* in any of those cycles anymore.

For you, maybe it's not sex or drugs or drinking. Maybe it's eating sweets. Maybe it's buying clothes. Maybe it's obsessing over a loss or constantly worrying about the future. Whatever it is, you do not have to stay stuck in the same hurtful behavior.

You *can* gain control over your life by regaining control of your mind through meditation. I can write it a million different ways, but all this book is about is your taking back your life and doing whatever it is you imagine!

The power that you'll gain through meditation will also help you get unstuck from whatever it is you perceive is holding you back from realizing your dreams.

Do you find yourself working extremely hard yet also feel like you're spinning your wheels professionally? Like no matter how much effort you apply, you're not "going anywhere"?

If so, the issue might be that you're not applying that effort in the space that's your true calling. Instead of listening to your dreams, you might be listening to the noise the world is putting in your ear.

Maybe it's the noise of your parents telling you, "Go to law school," even though in your heart, you want to be a painter. Or your uncle saying, "You need to take this custodian position I can get you. It's a good, safe union job," even though you've always dreamed about opening a recording studio. Or maybe it's even the guys on your corner saying, "Come on, you need to help us sell these rocks, how else are you going to make real money?" even though *you* have always wanted to go to law school.

When you move through life distracted, it becomes easy for those external voices to drown out the sound of your own dreams. But when you meditate, you will hear those dreams loud and clear and have the confidence to follow them, wherever they might take you.

Look at me. In the last year or so, I've basically turned my entire life upside down, physically and professionally. I'd lived in New York City for almost my entire life, and being a New Yorker had always seemed like a fundamental part of my identity. It's where my business was based. It's where my brothers live. It's where I'd always felt the most comfortable.

But sitting in meditation in my NYC apartment every morning, I realized I needed a change. At first I heard that message in a soft voice, but over the course of a couple of months it became louder and louder. Until I couldn't ignore it anymore.

And what that voice was telling me was that I needed to sell my homes in New York, shut down most of my offices, and move to Los Angeles.

The main reason that voice was telling me to move was to be closer to my children, who live in LA. But I realized I also wanted to try something new professionally. I've always been intrigued by Hollywood and how it impacts our culture, so I decided to throw my hat into that ring and see what happened. And as I'm writing this, I've already experienced tremendous success working with people like Chris Conte and Jay Stein at All Def Digital on new film and television projects. I'm at a stage professionally where some people have one eye on retirement, but I feel as energized as I did thirty years ago. As I like to say, "New shit keeps me young."

But I also know a lot of people in similar situations who wouldn't be able to make that move. Not because they don't want to try something new and shake up their lives a little bit, but because they feel like they've stopped evolving. If they're a fifty-year-old lawyer who's worked in the same firm for the last twenty years in Boston, they can't conceive that they could also be a fifty-one-year-old painter in Seattle. Or a restaurateur in New Orleans. In their minds, their identity is set. Whether that identity is making them happy or not.

It was the same way with switching careers. I know a lot of people who are incredibly successful and would love to get a fresh start but, again, are entangled in the anxiety that accompanies considering a change.

It's not that they couldn't support themselves financially through a transition period—a lot of these people are multimillionaires who could go years without earning a salary if they wanted to—but rather they are fearful about breaking the routine that they've developed over the years.

So much of their identity is tied up in their role at their firm, or their record label, or their company, that they choose to ignore that voice inside of them that tells them that they're no longer in love with what they're doing.

But if they were to sit down and meditate every day, I know that in a relatively short period of time that fear would begin to drift away. Instead of only seeing the perceived pitfalls and obstacles associated with change, their lens would clear up and instead they would begin to see all the excitement and possibilities that they could be experiencing.

When you sit in meditation every day, you are able to connect with what you are truly feeling about yourself. It puts you in touch with your true feelings in a very concrete way.

Again, this was what gave me the freedom to move to LA. Even if it took me some time to realize I needed a change professionally, meditation helped me hear what my heart was saying about my personal life. And what it was saying—very clearly—was, "You miss your daughters."

This is another wonderful benefit of meditation—it forces you to address and fix the relationships that are the most important to you.

Which is not to suggest that my relationship with my daughters needed fixing. Despite being on opposite coasts most of the time, we were very close—we Skyped several times a day, talked on the phone, and visited together every few weeks. But as much as I tried, I knew all that Skyping and flying back and forth wasn't the answer.

It wasn't the same as being able to pick them up from school or sit down at dinner with them and ask how their day was. When I was running around New York taking meetings or attending events, I could push that fact out of my mind, but when I was sitting there in meditation, there was no getting around it. But now that I pick my daughters up every morning and meditate with them from 6:45 to 7:05 before driving them to school, I know that I'm doing the right thing. I'm so grateful that I can feel the peace and happiness when we sit in silence together each morning.

I'm not trying to suggest that I'm somehow a better father than most people. I personally know of plenty of fathers who would like to be closer to their children, both physically and emotionally, but become anxious when they face the steps they would need to take to make it happen. Instead of moving to the sound of their heart, they feel stuck.

But when I thought about getting close to my kids and their mother, I didn't get stuck. If anxiety floated into my mind, I was able to watch it float right back out again.

The truth is that I love my kids and their mother, and thanks to meditation, I was able to stay focused on that truth instead of getting distracted by the fears that often accompany change.

When your mind is settled, the emotions that you have been

ignoring, that you're afraid that you aren't ready to deal with, are going to rise up to the surface. Whether it's emotions about your relationships, your job, your body, or anything you've been avoiding, the defense mechanism of fear that has been keeping that feeling suppressed is going to drift away. It's as if when you finally let down your guard during meditation, it's going to let all your dreams come up to the surface. And once they're there, you'll realize just how easy it is to follow them instead of staying stuck in place.

CHAPTER 16

MEDITATION OVER MEDICATION

I want to talk a moment here about one of the most vicious cycle people get caught up in, which is substance abuse.

Meditation is a powerful and effective way to deal with that abuse. Obviously substances like cocaine, alcohol, and even cigarettes are physically addictive, but studies have shown that meditation can help weaken that addiction.

A recent study by professors at Texas Tech and the University of Oregon found that people who were taught meditation reported a significant decrease in their craving for cigarettes. The findings were so encouraging that the researchers believe that meditation can be used to break not just nicotine cravings but all kinds of addiction. "Because mindfulness meditation promotes personal control and has been shown to positively affect attention and an openness to internal and external experiences, we believe that meditation may be helpful for coping with symptoms of addiction," Professor Yi-Yuan Tang of Texas Tech University told Science Newsline.

Those findings echo the results found by researchers at Yale, who also studied the effects of meditation on a group of nicotine addicts. Half the group was taught meditation; the other half was given the American Lung Association's "gold standard" treatment, which involves education and "nicotine replacement therapy," including gum, inhalers, and prescription drugs like Zyban and Chantix. The study found that the group trained in meditation had much greater success in giving up cigarettes than the group who relied on nicotine gum or prescription drugs. In their conclusion, the researchers wrote, "Mindfulness training may confer benefits greater than those associated with current standard treatments for smoking cessation."

But as anyone who's ever struggled with drugs or alcohol can tell you, it's not just a physical issue. The drugs might get you physically hooked, but the reason you turn to them in the first place is usually emotional. And this is where I feel meditation is particularly helpful in getting people unstuck. Or better yet, never even getting caught up in that cycle in the first place.

I *know* that the urge that drives a lot of people to drinking and drugs is a desire to quiet the noise in their head. Maybe it's the noise of anxiety. Or of depression. Or insecurity. Or doubt. Or sadness. Or sensitivity. Or hurt. Whatever it is, or wherever it comes from, people want it gone, and drugs seem to be the easiest way to make that happen.

Personally, I now see that when I used to get high, it was only because I wanted to drown out the noise. I was fortunate in that I never really felt depressed or sad, but I did hear the noise of anxiety.

So I tried to drown it out with drugs—weed, cocaine, heroin, and angel dust—as I've alluded to. Yes, the guy who doesn't even want to eat a bite of steak today, in no small part because of what it might do to his body, used to "get wet" (the term for smoking dust) without a second thought. I smoked so much dust back then that people used to talk openly about it in their songs, with Beastie Boys even rapping, "Our manager's crazy, he always smokes dust." Of course they also rhymed, "Had a caine-filled Kool with my man Rush Rush," so I guess I was smoking a lot of coke by then too.

The point is, back then it seemed like not only myself but a lot of the people I was running with were trying to quiet their noise with drugs. Which isn't surprising, because I was hanging with a lot of creative types—rappers, producers, musicians, artists, and writers—who seem particularly sensitive to the noise in their head.

Interestingly, the one person in our crew who never got high was Rick Rubin, who, as I mentioned, was taught meditation as a kid. Not too long ago an interviewer asked Rick how he managed to stay sober while working with so many artists who used drugs, and he had a very telling answer: "Everyone has their own way of coping and dealing with the world," he told *Purple* magazine. "I understand that the reason so many artists do drugs is that they're sensitive. I understand the need for self-medication. But I've done it more with meditation and therapy. Meditation is a way of seeking. I'm into

There is a really strong connection between the creativity musicians feel while working on new songs and meditation. Sting even said, "Yoga introduced me to a style of meditation. The only meditation I would have done before would be in the writing of songs."

So if you're a singer, musician, songwriter, or really any creative type looking for ways to get more in touch with your muse, I would urge you to start meditating. In the music world, a lot of people believe that the only way to get into that "zone" is through drugs or alcohol, but meditation can take you there too.

analyzing why things are the way they are. . . . If something is painful, if you're sensitive or uncomfortable, if you feel like you're different, your choices are to examine this and figure it out, or to numb yourself and ignore it. Most people tend to numb themselves and ignore their problems to avoid how they feel. Most people don't seek therapeutic help, and just look for ways to kill the pain. We live in a kill-the-pain society. TV kills the pain. Doctors prescribe drugs to kill the pain. Somehow I got into tuning into how I feel and trying to understand it."

Rick is a beautiful soul who believes in letting other people figure stuff out on their own, so he never really gave us a hard time about all the drugs we were doing. But it's clear to me in retrospect

Yes, they came into the rap game rhyming about partying and getting high, but in just a few years the Beasties had awakened to the power of meditation. If you're not already familiar, check out some of the lyrics to their song "Bodhisattva Vow," a reworking of the pledge Buddhists take to try to obtain enlightenment. To me, it's the realest shit they ever wrote.

that even at a young age he understood that meditation was a much better way to deal with your emotions than getting high.

Thankfully I figured that out too in time. As did, for that matter, the Beasties. Even back in 1992 they were writing songs like "Namaste" and "Bodhisattva Vow," with the lyrics "For the sake of all beings I seek / The enlightened mind that I know I'll reach." The group, especially my beautiful friend Adam Yauch, who left us way too soon, did so much to raise consciousness in this country about the power of meditation.

For creative types in particular, meditation can help you avoid so much of the suffering that inevitably comes from abusing drugs. Someone else who's experienced meditation's ability to break addictive cycles is the comedian Russell Brand. Russell is a brilliant guy who has been very courageous not only in speaking about his addiction but in working with the David Lynch Foundation to help other people struggling to turn their lives around through meditation.

In an essay he wrote for the UK's *Guardian*, Russell talked about why drugs helped him deal with the anxiety and hurt he was carrying around with him. "I cannot accurately convey to you the efficiency of heroin in neutralizing pain," he wrote. "It transforms a tight, white fist into a gentle, brown wave."

Unfortunately, the "gentle" wave never proves an easy one to ride, as Russell found out the hard way. At the height of his addiction he was using heroin and smoking crack every day, culminating in his getting fired from MTV for showing up to work on September 12, 2011, dressed as Osama bin Laden. He was that far gone.

Like me, Russell came to meditation through yoga. And like me as well, in meditation he quickly found a way to escape the noise that had been occupying his head for so many years. He said during a recent speech at the David Lynch Foundation that he was a committed drug addict for a long time, that he was really committed to that. Through meditation, he found this beautiful serenity. And a selfless connection. He had a tendency to selfishness and he felt that exposed as a superficial and pointless perspective to have. He felt love, for himself, but for everyone else too.

Russell's story is another reminder that no matter how rich or famous or successful someone is, if they feel isolated from the world due to the noise in their head, they're never going to be happy. That's why if you see an actor or athlete with a drug problem and think, "Why would they throw away all that money and fame for drugs?" the answer normally is because, as we've established, money and fame don't drown out the noise in their heads. These people might seem to "have it all," but the noise keeps them feeling separated from the world. Millions of fans might love them, their peers might respect and be lining up to work with them, but because of the noise in their own head, they can't feel any of that love. Physically they're always surrounded by other people, but emotionally they're isolated. So they try to deal with that noise by using drugs and alcohol.

I wish they knew—like Rick Rubin knows, like Russell Brand knows, like Alice Walker knows, and like Adam Yauch knew—that when you meditate, you're never going to feel isolated. Instead, you're always going to feel connected. Connected to the stillness in your heart and everyone else's.

CHAPTER 17

LIFE WITHOUT JUDGMENT

Another way that meditation will improve your life and relationship with the world is that it will make you less judgmental.

At first glance, becoming less judgmental might not seem to be such an important change to make in our lives. We tend to treat being judgmental as one of those areas where we could always stand to improve and not one that would ever really stand in the way of our sense of contentment or happiness.

Yet in reality being judgmental is often one of our biggest flaws as individuals, a trait that often represents one of the biggest barriers between us and the happiness that we seek.

Think about how much time we waste every day being judgmental toward other people over things they have no control over. What am I talking about? Criticizing people for being short, bald people for losing their hair, and even old people for being wrinkled.

Not to mention how we waste a tremendous amount of time judging people for the types of clothes that they wear, the music that they listen to, how they style their hair, the brand of sneaker they wear, the type of car that they drive, or the neighborhood they live in. And the list could go on and on.

Ultimately, all those wasteful judgments are rooted in our own insecurities, right? We judge bald people because we're worried about losing our own hair, we look down on people's cars because we're insecure about what we're driving ourselves, and we try to avoid old people because we're fearful of growing old and dying ourselves.

Personally, I used to suffer very badly from these sorts of attitudes. I was quick to judge people over anything. From downright silly stuff, like the fact that their sneakers didn't match their shirt, to whether or not someone was "cool" enough to be seen at the party with or whether they were "smart enough" to go into business with.

But after meditation helped clear my lenses, I was able to see that the only reason I was so judgmental was because I was insecure about myself. I was anxious about my own choices and abilities, and I was projecting that insecurity onto the people I'd encounter in life.

I'll give you an example: Before I started meditating, I would get very anxious about the idea of doing live TV. I was filled with fear that as soon as I opened my mouth, no matter what I was saying, people were going to judge me. And their verdict was going to be that I was an idiot.

Remember Def Comedy Jam, when I used to come out at the end of the show and say, "God bless and good night"? I used to get so filled with anxiety when it was time for me to go out that the producers would literally have to push me onstage just to say those four simple words.

Which is to say nothing of actually going on TV and talking about an issue. It got to the point where my assistants would turn down TV interviews without even checking with me first because they knew I'd say no. I'd even try to get out of speaking at galas or award shows where I was the person being honored. The organizers of those events probably thought I had an attitude or too much ego, but I was too anxious about the thought of standing up and speaking in front of a room full of people.

After I started meditating, all that anxiety just drifted away. Sure, I'd still have moments where I'd be afraid of making a critical mistake on TV, but they would pass very quickly. Instead of stressing over how I'd be judged if I said the wrong thing, I just reminded myself, "Who cares?" and realized that I had nothing to worry about. Don't get me wrong, I'm sure people have seen me on TV and thought, "What is Russell talking about?" or "He's not making sense," but if that's how they feel, then that's how they feel. The important thing is that I'm not entangled in judging myself anymore. Because I know that when I speak, I'm speaking from the heart, and for every person who judges me negatively, there are many more who hear me talking about gun violence, education reform, or the abuse of animals and are positively affected by what I have to say.

There's no doubt that meditation will clear off your lenses that have been dirtied by years and years of anxiety and allow you to see the best in yourself. But just as important, when you finally put down all the judgment you've been carrying around with you, instead of focusing on people's perceived weaknesses, you'll start seeing all the *good* they're bringing to the table.

This is so important. Imagine how much better your life would be if you moved through it only taking the *good* from people. Because usually when we meet someone with negative energy or perspectives that we view as harmful, the negativity is what we hold on to. Their perceived negativity is how we come to define those people. But in the end, who does that hurt? Those people probably aren't changing their energy, but we're still stuck holding on to their negativity. Often even long after they've left our lives and stopped thinking about us.

But when judgment is taken out of your heart, you can look past those people's negativity, which is probably just a reflection of their anxiety, and see whatever is good in them. Even if it seems like 90 percent of what they give the world is filled with anger and hurt, if you can focus on that loving 10 percent of them hidden behind the bluster, then you're going to get the best of that relationship. At the very least *you're* not going to be burdened by *their* negativity. And you never know, but often by focusing on that loving 10 percent, you'll actually have a chance to change some of their more negative views.

For instance, a lot of people wonder how I can have relationships with right-wing pundits like Bill O'Reilly or Sean Hannity. I certainly don't agree with their politics or their takes on society. But despite our differences, I try not to *judge* them. Instead, I try to take the positive from them, even if at times it might seem hard to find, and build on that. You see, personalities like Bill O'Reilly and Sean Hannity are always going to have a pulpit. They, or people very similar to them, are always going to be in a position to influence others and shape opinion. So rather than dismiss them out of hand, I try to find those small spaces where we at least agree to disagree and then build on that. Because if I can have a dialogue and reach even just a few members of their audience with my message, instead of judging them and writing them all off as bigots or blowhards, then maybe I can effect some positive change. Which is a lot healthier for myself and for society.

But I'll be real: I'm only able to have a relationship with an O'Reilly or a Hannity because I'm not anxious about what people think of me. In the past, I would have been nervous about how people on the left would have perceived my going on a show like O'Reilly's. Would they call me a sellout? An apologist? A fool? Now I'm not wrapping myself up in knots worrying about the answers to those questions. Instead, I'm perfectly comfortable with them. I know exactly where my heart is at and exactly what I'm trying to accomplish. I'm not going to engage any judgment that might be thrown my way.

I've been talking about how the letting go of judgment has helped me personally, but I also want to stress how letting go of judgment can help us as a society. Or to take it even a step farther, how it can help heal mankind.

Because if we look at the prejudices that hurt us collectively, that are holding us down all across the globe, they're all born out of judgment too.

Racism.

Homophobia.

Sexism.

Religious intolerance.

Ageism.

Classism.

They are all rooted in judgment.

We already know the terrible price the victims of these judgments pay, but let's all consider how much it's hurting the people doing the judgment.

Not to sound too sympathetic for people practicing racism or homophobia, but the truth is, carrying around that sort of judgment in your own heart is an incredible burden in life. If you're walking around worried about someone else's sexuality or how they pray to God, you're living a fundamentally unhappy life.

And I'm not only talking about over-the-top examples like the Ku Klux Klan, homophobes, or religious fundamentalists, but everyday folk like you and me who, despite what we might say publicly or even tell ourselves, still carry around judgment for people we perceive as different from ourselves.

I've certainly been guilty of it in the past. Making little jokes about people who might look, pray, or love differently than I did. It wasn't an impossible weight for me to carry, but it was enough to keep me from reaching my highest heights. My greatest potential.

Some 2,500 years ago, Lord Buddha came up with a very succinct way to describe the dangers of judgment. "You will not be punished for your anger," he taught. "You will be punished *by* your anger." It's still true today. Think about that the next time you feel yourself about to engage in racism, sexism, homophobia, or any type of intolerance.

But I promise you meditation has helped cleanse almost *all* of that judgment from my heart. And the really incredible thing that I've learned is that when you move all that judgment out of your heart, it's not just like that space sits there empty. No, when you get rid of the judgment, what actually replaces it is compassion.

And compassion is actually one of the most powerful tools you can use in life. Too often in our society we view compassion and friendliness as weaknesses. Almost, as we might say in hip-hop, as "some sucka shit." Nothing, however, could be farther from the truth. A truly compassionate person is as strong as a rock. A person who moves through life focused on friendship and empathy will actually be one of the hardest people you'll ever met. As it says in the Yoga Sutras, *"Maitryadisu balani,"* or "The cultivation of friendliness creates inner strength."

It's ironic, because we've come to accept collectively that the self-centered, egotistical person is the one who will "get more" out of life. It's true, they might get more material goods, or money, or sex, or power. But they will not get happiness. No, for self-centered, egotistical people, happiness actually proves very elusive.

But for the compassionate and empathetic person, happiness is almost guaranteed. If you can let go of judgment and move through life only thinking of how you can relate to and help the people you meet, you're going to make them very happy. And their happiness will in turn bring you a type of joy and contentedness you probably haven't experienced before.

CHAPTER 18

THE POWER OF COMPASSION

I f you haven't noticed, I like to mix it up a bit when it comes to religion. I think Buddhism, Christianity, Hinduism, Judaism, and so many other faiths are all great. But at the end of the day, even though I love them all, I don't consider myself a follower of any of those things.

Instead, whenever someone asks me what religion I follow, I reply, "My religion is compassion."

To me, compassion is the ultimate expression of your highest self. When you realize that you are completely connected to everyone and everything on the planet—including the animals—this is when you have truly lived up to your full potential.

The irony is, when I look around at a lot of so-called religious leaders today, I don't see a lot of compassion. I see a lot of judgment and even

"If you want others to be happy, practice compassion. If you want to be happy, practice compassion."
—The Dalai Lama

hatred, but not so much empathy. But the great prophets these people claim they follow—Jesus, Muhammad, Buddha, and Abraham—were all *extremely* compassionate individuals.

It's almost as if all these great faiths were built around the idea of compassion thousands of years ago and since then we've collectively drifted further and further away from that ideal.

Meditation, thankfully, can help bring us back to it.

Even though Buddhists in particular have been saying for thousands of years that meditation promotes compassion, modern studies are now proving it too.

In the 1990s, the Dalai Lama began taking adepts—a term for Buddhist monks who had meditated for at least ten thousand hours—to Western scientists to see if there was a way to measure meditation's effect on compassion.

So researchers at the University of Wisconsin conducted a study where they monitored the brain waves of those monks and compared them to the brain waves of a group of people who had just been taught how to meditate.

Both the monks and the control group were asked to meditate

on the concept of compassion and were monitored both while they were meditating and after they'd stopped.

What the study found was that during meditation both the monks and the novice meditators experienced increased gamma brain waves, which the scientists associated with compassionate thoughts. But when they stopped meditating on compassion, the novices' gamma waves slowed down, while the monks' kept growing stronger. To the researchers, this was proof that all those thousands of hours in meditation had actually trained those monks' brains to be more compassionate.

Another fascinating study illustrating the link between meditation and compassion was recently conducted by researchers from Northeastern University and Harvard. In that study, a control group was taught meditation for several weeks. After they finished, they were each asked to go to a fake doctor's office and observed to see if they would get up and offer their seat when a person (really an actor) in obvious pain and on crutches entered the waiting room and didn't have anywhere to sit down.

The study found that only 15 percent of people who hadn't been taught meditation got up and offered their seat to the person on crutches. But out of the group that had been taught meditation, 50 percent of the people got up.

The results were so striking that in announcing the findings, Northeastern University released a statement saying, "These results appear to prove what the Buddhist theologians have long believed—that meditation is supposed to lead you to experience more compassion and love for all sentient beings."

This is a really big deal. Again, if you were to make a list of aspects of yourself that you wanted to improve, compassion might not be at the top of the list. But it should be.

That's because when you're compassionate, you're not only connected but grateful as well. And a connected and grateful person is *extremely* attractive to the world.

Think about it: Who's the most compassionate and grateful person that you know? Someone who, no matter what the situation, goes out of their way to try to make everyone around them feel good and comfortable. Someone who, no matter what you do for them (or even don't do), always goes out of their way to tell you that they appreciated what you did for them, or appreciated that you *tried* to do it. Someone who's going to lend a helping hand whether they've known you for ten minutes or for ten years.

Maybe it's someone at your church. Or on your block. Or at your job. Whoever that person is in your life, I bet they're successful. They might not be "rich," but I bet they're respected at what they do. I bet that if you ever had a business you wanted to start or a great opportunity fell into your lap, they're one of the people you'd want to partner up with. I bet when their boss has to make a tough decision, that compassionate person is the one they turn to for advice and insight.

I know that's how my office operates. I always look to surround myself with compassionate people. Simone Reyes, who's worked alongside of me for over twenty-five years, is one of the most compassionate people I've ever met. When she's not helping me run my business and charities, she's an incredibly dedicated animal rights activist. She's a hard-core supporter of organizations like PETA, Mercy for Animals, Farm Sanctuary, and Animal Acres. Her passion for reminding people that we need to be compassionate toward animals inspires me every day.

Michael Skolnik, who is my political director and runs my website Global Grind, is also an incredibly compassionate individual. Perhaps as much as anyone I know, every day Michael wakes up focused on how he can help alleviate other people's suffering. For Michael, that compassion often expresses itself in his work speaking out against gun violence. From his role in demanding justice for Trayvon Martin to his work in the streets of Queens, Michael has dedicated so much of his time to not only stopping future violence but providing support to families who have suffered the unspeakable tragedy of losing a loved one to guns.

Now, since I'm a "hip-hop mogul," you probably figure that my inner circle consists of a bunch of lawyers, Ivy League BAs, and number guys. Nope. I can promise you that my most trusted advisers are an animal rights activist and a gun violence activist. Not to mention a rabbi and a Muslim imam. Because in their compassion, I see incredible strength and integrity. Values that mean much more to me as a boss than any degree on a wall or bottom line on a spreadsheet.

One of the most inspiring examples of meditation's ability to increase compassion comes from an unlikely source: the US Army. Workers at a VA center in Menlo Park, California, recently hooked up with teachers at Stanford to put veterans through a course called

"Compassion Cultivation Training." The program helps vets coming back from places like Iraq and Afghanistan who are suffering from PTSD, or post-traumatic stress disorder.

Specifically, a lot of those vets were stationed in areas where they'd been taught to view civilians as potential threats. And when they returned home, they couldn't deactivate that way of thinking. Whereas before they were viewing Iraqis or Afghanis as threats, now they were looking at their own neighbors, even their own wives and children, that way. And it wasn't just recent vets. The VA works with a lot of soldiers who came back from Vietnam thirty-five years ago and are still dealing with these same issues.

In the program, the soldiers sit in meditation and focus on the phrase "That person is just like me." One of the program's founders, Leah Weiss of Stanford, tells NPR that the process allows vets to let go of a lot of the fear and distrust they've been carrying around with them. It allows them to remember that, "just like me, this person's had ups and downs in his or her life. Just like me, this person's had goals and dreams."

John Perry, a Vietnam vet, told NPR that meditating helped him come to terms with pain and anxiety he'd been carrying around for decades. "It's pretty much a self-imposed prison," he said. "I didn't talk to anyone. No one would ask me any questions about [the war]. I wouldn't answer if they did. So isolation has been my problem for forty years."

One of the main reasons I'm so committed to the David Lynch Foundation is their dedication to using meditation to help veterans.

They even committed a million dollars toward starting a program called Operation Warrior Wellness that teaches Transcendental Meditation to returning vets. My great friend Bob Roth, who runs the organization, has been teaching meditation to veterans for years but recently told CNN's Soledad O'Brien (who also practices TM), "It's just been in the past years where [there's] the understanding that post-traumatic stress disorder is a real epidemic that has no conventional, traditional solution." Bob adds that research has shown that meditation can promote a 50 percent reduction in the symptoms of PTSD.

Obviously the need to reconnect with compassion is most severe in vets, but the truth is that we all suffer from this sense of isolation to a certain degree. We're born filled up with compassion, but the older we get, it's almost as if it starts to slowly leak out of us. Next time you're around little kids, notice how quick they are to hug someone who's feeling sad. Or how when one kid feels bad, they all start to feel bad. That sense of communal compassion is at our essence as humans. But the farther we move through life, the more we lose that connection. We begin to get so caught up in our own perceived suffering that we forget about what other people are going through too. Meditation brings us back to that childlike sense of connectedness.

Never underestimate the impact increased compassion can have on your life. In fact, let me let the Dalai Lama have the final word on this topic:

"Compassion is the ultimate source of success in life," he writes. "I believe that at every level of society—familial, tribal, national, and international—the key to a happier and more successful world is the growth of compassion. We do not need to become religious, nor do we need to believe in an ideology. All that is necessary is for each of us to develop our good human qualities. . . . I try to treat whoever I meet as an old friend. This gives me a genuine feeling of happiness. It is the practice of compassion."

PART FIVE

How to Meditate

CHAPTER 19

TRUST THE PROCESS

N ow that I've spent so much time hyping up the benefits of meditation, you're probably thinking that the actual process must be elaborate. Something that's going to bring you increased happiness, health, focus, creativity, balance, and compassion, to say nothing of helping foster world peace, must be complicated, right?

Nope.

In fact, the practice of meditation is about as simple and effortless as it gets. All it involves is sitting for twenty minutes twice a day with your eyes closed.

That's it.

Unlike practices like lifting weights, working out, or running that require special equipment or a dedicated space, you literally don't need *anything* to meditate.

That's right. As I told you earlier, you don't need a special "meditation room" with a mat on the floor, the curtains pulled shut, and incense burning. And even though some people find them helpful, you don't really need special meditation benches or cushions either.

All you "need" is a comfortable seat. No bells, no whistles, no machines, no fancy clothes or special workout gear. Just you, your mind, and a seat. (I put "need" in quotations because the truth is you don't even really need anywhere particular to sit. Remember, Lord Buddha became enlightened while meditating sitting under a tree, so even a chair, let alone a "meditation room," is a bit of a Western luxury.)

Having said that, I understand that for beginners, it isn't always easy to sit down, close your eyes, and quickly settle into a state of stillness. No, your thoughts have gotten used to making too much noise to just shut up. They have enjoyed too much influence over you to simply fade away the first time you sit down and close your eyes. That's why now I want to walk you through the actual steps of meditation that will allow you to naturally and effortlessly transcend thinking. That will allow you to step out of your stressful world and into a restful state of deep consciousness.

The technique I'm about to describe reflects the influence of several different approaches I've learned over the years directly from masters like Bob Roth, who espouses Transcendental Meditation, and the yoga masters David Life and Sharon Gannon.

I've also incorporated lessons and styles I've learned from various other experts I've meditated with and studied under during my many trips around the world.

I'll admit that a few more "orthodox" meditators might not approve of my mixing up so many styles, but frankly, if you know anything about me, then you know I rarely take an orthodox or traditional approach to doing things!

I've already shared this technique with countless friends and they've gotten tremendous value out of it. Some of them really responded to the mantra and ended up being inspired to take the actual TM course, which is highly recommended to anyone who is interested. Others told me that they really connected to the yoga elements and were inspired to explore that practice, which is beautiful too.

In order for this journey to lead you to the power and peace inside your heart, it is critical that you trust the prescription I'm about to share with you now. I don't say that out of ego, but rather out of the understanding that to be a successful student, you must accept your teacher. If you adhere to my authority in following these instructions, I can promise you that all of the attributes we've mentioned will blossom in your own life. What I am about to open is a gateway to the easiest person.

YOUR SEAT

The first step in meditating is finding a peaceful spot where you can sit in silence for twenty minutes. If it's a quiet place where there aren't a lot of distractions, that's great. But if there's some noise going on around you, don't let that get you bent out of shape.

As I mentioned early on in the book, a major mistake a lot of beginners make is claiming that they don't have anywhere quiet to meditate and then giving up on the practice before they ever really get started. If you hear the dog barking next door or a car alarm going off down the street, don't stress over it. Those noises will fade away from your mind, so don't use them as an excuse.

The point is, noise will only distract you if you let it. And unless you live in a monastery (in which case you probably aren't going to be reading this guide anyway), chances are you're going to hear some noises during your session. So take a second, listen to them, and rather than get frustrated by them, accept them as part of the world. Let go of any negative emotions you might have toward them and realize that they can't touch or affect your stillness. Noise should never be seen as an obstacle between you and your ability to meditate.

Some people, especially those who live in big cities like New York, have asked me about whether or not it's okay to use headphones or earplugs to block out distractions while they meditate. If you find that noises are distracting you to the point where you want to give up the practice, then I suppose it's okay to use headphones or earplugs to get more comfortable. Just remember that ultimately they are crutches—something you should only use until you're able to "walk" on your own again. You never want to rely on them in order to meditate.

This is because the goal of your practice is to take the sense of stillness and peace you experience during meditation and carry it with you as you move through the world. A world that is usually pretty noisy. So unless you plan on wearing earplugs during the rest of your day, I don't think it's in your best interest to meditate with them either. It's much healthier to learn how to not only live with but also embrace those distractions.

Okay, now that we've got the distractions out of the way, let's get down to the nitty-gritty: how you actually sit.

Some say the optimal way to sit during meditation is in what is known as the Lotus Pose. In the Lotus, you sit on the floor with your legs crossed, placing your right feet and ankles over your left thigh and your left feet and ankles over your right thigh.

If that's too difficult for you at first, you can start with the Half Lotus, in which you place your left leg over your right thigh but place your right foot under your left thigh (you can put whichever leg you prefer on top), which won't force you to stretch your body quite as much.

The reason the Lotus is considered by many to be the optimal pose is because when you are sitting with a straight back, it opens up your chest. And when your back is straight and your chest is open, it literally puts you in position to be open to all of life's blessings.

If you look at all the statues, carvings, and paintings of people meditating that have come from places like Japan, China, Tibet, India, and Nepal over the last several thousand years, you'll see that everyone is sitting with a very similar posture: back straight, chest

CHAIR MEDITATION

If you choose to begin this way, make sure you use a straight-backed wooden chair, rather than an office chair that's going to lean back, or a sofa chair or love seat. This is because you want to keep a straight back during your meditation, which is much easier on a wooden chair than on something soft that's going to let you sink into it. If you feel like you're having trouble keeping your back straight, try sitting on a small pillow so that your butt is a little bit higher than your knees. Once you're seated, gently push the back of your thighs and your sitz bones (the bones in your butt that you sit on) into the chair while gently pushing your feet into the ground. This is going to help you open up your chest and elongate your spine, which is the basic posture you want to maintain while you're meditating.

Even though you are sitting in a chair, do not allow yourself to lean against the back of the chair while you're meditating. You really want to focus on keeping your back straight with as little external support as possible. In time you'll be comfortable sitting without any support and then can transition into one of the Lotus poses. To make sure your head is in the right position, imagine a piece of string running from the base of your spine up through the top of your head and then all the way into the heavens. If that string feels slack or loose, then you could be in better alignment. But if that imaginary string seems taut, like you're hanging from a hook in the sky, then you've got it. And remember, just as your spirit has no choice but to evolve upward during meditation, it's the same for your spine. Even if you start off slouching, your natural tendency is going to be to straighten yourself out.

Also, make sure your hands are resting gently, not balled up into fists or in any way tight. You can place them palms down on your thighs if you're in a chair. If you're in the Lotus, you can rest them palms up on your thighs

Finally, allow your shoulders to become relaxed. A lot of times we think that our shoulders are relaxed and fluid, but we are actually holding a lot of tension there. (This is why we instinctively start rubbing people's shoulders when we think they're stressed out.) So to be sure you're not holding any stress while you meditate, simply roll your shoulders a few times and then let them gently settle.

open, and hands resting on their legs. That's the posture you could and should be moving toward in your practice. I actually keep several little statues of Buddha meditating around my house just to remind me of how I should be sitting, even if I'm not always in that perfect alignment.

That's the goal. But the reality is that almost no one ever gets it totally right. In some yoga practices it's even taught that if you were ever able to sit up perfectly straight you would become completely enlightened and turn into a ball of light. And you don't see many balls of light walking around, do you?

Instead, you probably see a lot of people walking around hunched over with bad posture. This is because most Americans aren't very flexible. So simply sitting straight for twenty minutes could prove to be difficult for the average reader at first. If you fall into that category, then don't feel as though you have to start in the Lotus at first. If sitting in a chair while you meditate feels better, then please do that! (See sidebar for more tips on meditating in a chair.) I don't want anyone reading this to stress over not being able to sit in one of the Lotus positions right away. As long as you're sitting without any affliction or discomfort for twenty minutes, then you're on the right road.

But no matter how inflexible you feel when you start meditating, I believe that over time you find yourself moving toward the Lotus position that I've prescribed. For example, I have a good friend who I taught how to meditate a few years ago. The first time we practiced, I had him sit in the half Lotus position on my living room floor. After five minutes, he knew there was no way he could hold that position and simply got up and continued his meditation sitting in a chair. He was a little embarrassed after the twenty minutes were over, as if he'd somehow "messed up," but I told him, "No, that was perfect. You must be comfortable when you meditate, so if you need to sit in a chair, then do it!"

So for the next few years, my friend continued to meditate in a chair. Being a writer, he'd spent years hunched over computer screens or slouching on sofas, and sitting with a straight back actually felt weird to him. All that sitting and slouching had literally gotten his spine bent out of shape and his body knocked out of alignment. So even though sitting up straight is the natural way we're supposed to sit (look at a little kid sitting on a kindergarten rug—they're almost always sitting straight up), it can actually feel *unnatural* until we reacquaint ourselves with it.

My friend got a lot of value out of meditating in a chair—he felt more rested, balanced, and at peace with himself even after just a few days of meditating. And as a writer, he was also really excited to see that his creativity and focus improved almost immediately after starting.

But he told me that several months ago he started to become very aware of how he was slouching while he meditated, how his spine felt compacted and his belly felt as though he were just hanging over his belt. He had become aware that he didn't want to feel that way when he sat—in meditation or otherwise—so he decided to try the Lotus again. And once again it felt "too hard." But this time, he decided to address his lack of flexibility and poor posture instead of ignoring it. He started taking yoga classes to learn how to lengthen his body and sit more easily. He started stretching more when he went to the gym.

And after several months of working on his flexibility and posture, he found that he was able to meditate in the Lotus position. And he found himself reaping even more benefits from his meditation. Which is not to say that he was "wasting his time" or "doing something wrong" those first few years he was meditating in a chair. In fact, he did exactly what he was supposed to do: He listened to his body.

His body told him that sitting with a straight spine was too hard at first, so he didn't push it. And then when his body told it was interested in trying to correct itself, he listened to it again and began that transition.

So no matter what type of seat, Lotus or the chair, you choose to begin your practice in, understand that you've made the right choice.

YOUR MANTRA

Once you've settled in to your seat, it's time to embrace your mantra. "Mantra" is a Sanskrit (one of the ancient languages of India) term, for which there are a lot of different definitions. I like the one that was taught to me by Deepak Chopra, who told me that in Sanskrit "*man*" equals "to think" and "*tra*" equals "tool" or "instrument." So we should think of a mantra as a tool to help us transcend the noise in our minds.

Now, when I give you your mantra shortly, it's going to look like a word. But it's not. Because while *this* mantra has a sound, it doesn't have a meaning. And the reason we're not going to use a mantra with a meaning is because if you are thinking about what your mantra means while you are saying it, then that's just another distraction your mind has to deal with before it can be truly resting or being still.

Look at it this way: If English is your native language and you say the word "elephant," then you're going to think of a big four-legged creature with a long trunk every time you say the word. Even if you tell your mind not to, you are still going to see that creature in your thoughts. But if someone were to say the Chinese word for "elephant," you wouldn't have any association for that sound. So you could hear it over and over again without actually picturing an elephant.

You need to take the same approach to your mantra. When we put associations on words or sounds, they become static. In order to help you reach the depths of the stillness that lies within you, your relationship with your mantra must be fluid and free at all times.

The mantra I'm going to share with you now is what's called a "mass mantra." It was taught to me by a master who explained that it was one of the mantras that works best for the widest range of people and particularly because it is gentle on adults' nervous systems. It's a mantra that has been used for thousands of years, so by using it, you will be entering into a collective experience that has been shared by literally hundreds of thousands—probably millions—of other people.

And the mantra is "rum."

Now, when you see the word "rum" on the page, it probably means something to you.

Whatever associations you have with the word "rum," let them go. In fact, try to stop thinking of it as a word at all. Instead, just think of it as a vibration. Remember, words are static. Vibrations are free.

And in meditation, you always want to be free.

So once you are seated in your seat and comfortable, say it out loud one time:

Rum.

Good. Now, say it another time, very loudly.

RUM.

Then repeat it quietly several times: rum rum rum.

Inhale deeply and say it once with a long vibration until you're almost out of breath.

Ruuuuuuuuuuuuuuuuuum.

Then try saying it with different emphases.

Rummmmm.

Ruuuuuuuuuuuum.

RUmm.

RuMMM.

Once you've said it so many times that you're starting to feel silly doing that, gently close your eyes. Then pick whatever version of "rum" feels most comfortable and start repeating it gently again, only this time not out loud but in your mind.

Now your meditation has begun.

DEALING WITH DISTRACTIONS

As you keep repeating your mantra, staying focused on "rum" might be harder than you anticipated. For example, you might find yourself getting physically distracted. Your arm might start to itch. At first it might just be a vague sensation, but the longer you go without scratching it, that itch might feel like it's getting louder and louder. You'll be trying to focus on the mantra but your thoughts will keep coming back to that itchy arm.

In some practices you'll be taught to try to ignore that itch. To try to shut it out of your mind by focusing even harder on your mantra or your breathing.

But I believe that if you feel an itch, then it's okay to scratch it.

I have been taught, and have found it to be true, that the distraction you create by trying to ignore that itch is actually greater than the distraction created by just scratching it real quick and then letting it go.

Because as your mantra helps you sink deeper and deeper into the peace of your heart, you'll have less and less interest in the distractions. To the point where mosquitoes could be biting you, your phone could be ringing off the hook, or Mister Softee could be parked right outside your window, but those distractions just won't seem important enough for you to address. As you begin to transcend your thoughts, the very idea of scratching an itch or worrying about a noise will seem like too big an expenditure of energy.

The reason you will become more attracted to the stillness than to the distractions is because your mind's natural inclination is to go to the most peaceful, restful place possible. Just like water always runs downstream, your mind naturally always wants to flow to a tranquil place. It might not seem that way—if anything, it might seem like your mind is predisposed to move toward noise and distraction—but it's the truth. And meditation will help you see that truth clearly.

If you learn anything from meditation, let it be that being peaceful and restful is actually your natural state. By spending so much time focused on the distractions of life, you've essentially been asking water to run upstream. Which is why at times life can feel so *hard*. Meditation is about getting rid of those distractions and letting the water follow its natural course again. Away from the noise and the distractions and back into your heart.

YOUR THOUGHTS

The greatest distractions you're going to face during meditation probably won't be physical ones like an itch or a sound, but rather the distractions caused by your own thoughts.

This is because as you begin to repeat your mantra, your thoughts are going to become agitated. Especially if you're a novice. And it's because they're jealous.

That's right, your thoughts are going to become jealous of your mantra. And you can't really blame them. After all, they've enjoyed free rein in your mind for years and years. They've come and gone as they pleased, been as loud as they want to be, sometimes even refusing to quiet down at bedtime. They've had complete run of the place.

Now all of a sudden here comes this mantra entering their territory without permission. And even worse, it won't back down. It's not aggressive or confrontational, but it just keeps coming and coming at the same steady, gentle pace. Ruuum. Ruuum. Ruuum. Ruuum. Ruuum. So of course your thoughts are going to take exception and try to be even louder than usual.

If you've ever struggled with insomnia, it's similar to that. When you're lying there awake in the middle of the night, it seems like it's impossible to shut your thoughts off. Going back to sleep is clearly what's in everyone's best interest, but your thoughts aren't trying to be good teammates. Instead, it seems like they actually enjoy keeping you awake. It can be four A.M. and you know that if you don't get back to sleep you're going to be a mess at work the next morning, but your thoughts will keep coming in waves, reminding you about everything from trivial little things around the house to big, emotional issues about your relationships and life.

So just like an insomniac's thoughts fight back when he tries to go to sleep, your thoughts might begin to push back when your mantra first appears. As you keep saying "ruuuum," a thought about an e-mail you forgot to respond to might enter your head. It might be a pushy, aggressive thought that fights very loudly to make itself heard over your mantra.

Whatever you do, don't "fight" that thought. Don't squinch up your face and try to make that thought go away by concentrating even harder on your mantra. Or even worse, don't get wrapped up thinking about that e-mail and then suddenly realize, "Man, I've totally forgotten about my mantra. This isn't working today. I'm going to stop meditating and try again tomorrow." Please don't do that. I don't care if you get lost in that thought about an e-mail for five minutes; when you realize that you have, simply let that thought go and then gently bring your mantra back to the forefront of your mind.

Whatever thought comes into your mind after that, just consider it for a moment and then gently return to your mantra again. The cycle I just described might happen five times, it might happen ten times or might feel like it's happening for the entire twenty minutes you are sitting in meditation. But no matter how big a fight your thoughts put up, *always* let your mind drift back to your meditation.

To help people better understand this process, I like to use the very simple analogy that your mind is like a cage and your thoughts are like a monkey. When you first sit down and close your eyes, that monkey is going to act up. He's going to start jumping around, making crazy monkey sounds, maybe even start throwing shit at you. Hey, that's just how monkeys do.

But if you don't engage that monkey, if you don't scream back at him and show him that you're rattled, eventually that monkey is going to lose interest. Instead of making noise or throwing shit, he'll wander off and become quiet. It might take a couple or even five minutes. Just know that however long it takes, your mantra will always tame that monkey.

You must accept that no matter how loud the distractions seem at first, as long as you stick with your mantra, eventually you won't hear them anymore.

If you're still having trouble with this concept, consider a final analogy. Have you ever spent the night in a room with one of those old-fashioned alarm clocks? The ones where you can hear every tick-tock? If so, then you know that when you first try to go to sleep, that ticking next to your head sounds *extremely* loud. You might even think, "There's no way I'm ever going to be able to fall asleep with this clock ticking in my ear."

But after several minutes of being distracted, your thoughts begin to settle and gradually the ticking doesn't seem to lower in volume. Before long you can't even hear it at all and you drift off to sleep.

It's not that the noise ever went away. That ticking was just as loud when you first lay down as when you eventually went to sleep. It's just that as you became more restful, the sound didn't seem so loud anymore.

During meditation, your thoughts are going to be just like that alarm clock. They're never going to go away, unless you reach a very advanced stage of enlightenment. Instead, the more peaceful and restful you become, the less and less you'll actually notice them. As your thoughts settle, they will become less and less intrusive.

Whatever you do, try not to get bent out of shape or frustrated when you still hear some thoughts in your mind. If your thoughts are getting too loud, again, gently let your mantra replace them. As long as you do it effortlessly, then you're doing it the "right" way. Even if you never end up returning to your mantra, just by letting your thoughts settle you will be giving your nervous system a chance to calm down, which will promote physical healing. This is why as long as you stay sitting in silence, the only "wrong" thing you can do during meditation is somehow try to "fight" or correct what you're experiencing.

TAKING INVENTORY

As your thoughts begin to settle, you'll begin to experience the first stage of meditation, which is known as "quieter thought." Or as I like to call it, "taking inventory." During this stage, any thought that does come into your head will appear so slowly and serenely that you'll be able to consider it in a way that you never could normally. It's as if the smudge of the world has been wiped off your lenses and you can finally see your ideas cleanly and clearly. This stage is when you'll encounter some of your most creative ideas and impulses.

When Russell Brand talked about having a million-dollar idea during meditation, I'm sure it came during this "inventory" stage, just as many of my most creative ideas, especially, as I've mentioned, the ones I've had for my film and TV companies, have come during this stage. Because when I'm taking inventory, I'm still seeing my thoughts, but now it's as if it's from a distance. And taking my ego out of my mind is what's created that distance.

When I say "ego," I'm not using the word the way it's often used these days, which is to describe a certain kind of "confidence" or "cockiness." When I say "ego," I'm taking about your *false* sense of self.

That part of your mind where all the needless fear, greed, judgment, inflexibility, anger, and resentment that you might experience come from. A part of your mind that tells you—falsely—that you have to act a certain way, live a certain way, even think a certain way in order to be okay. This is why my brother Reverend Run likes to say that "ego" stands for "Edging God Out." When you let the anxiety, neediness, and greed take up all the space in your mind, you are edging out your true self.

But as you repeat your mantra, that ego will begin to dissipate. Basically, all the BS that you've let pile up in your mind will disappear and all that will be left are your good thoughts. Your pure thoughts. The thoughts that reflect how you *truly* feel about your life, rather than the thoughts that reflect what you think you should feel, the view that lets you trust in the perfection in the world. These are the thoughts that are going to show you the right decision to make with your career. With your marriage. With your relationship with your children. With the world.

Again, these are those "pearls of right solutions" we keep speaking of. And the "inventory" stage is the right time to pick them.

So don't try to rush through the inventory stage or get frustrated because you're "still" experiencing thoughts despite repeating your mantra. Instead, consider these thoughts. Not every one of them is going to make you a million dollars or help you make an important life choice, but the more time you spend taking inventory, day in and day out, the more familiar you will become with your true self.

The self that moves through life free of envy, anger, greed, and hatred and instead is able to live up to its full potential.

You'll also find yourself taking inventory of your body in this stage. If you have a bad habit of slouching, you will be aware of it during this stage. If your belly is starting to get a little big, you will be aware of it during this stage. If you have a chronic tightness in your back or your ankle, you will be aware of it during this stage.

It's not that you didn't already know that you tend to slouch or that your belly is getting softer, but you've been putting off dealing with those facts. Or if you do address them, it's with a distracted mind, one that filters them through a prism of anxiety or sadness. Which is why people will look in the mirror, see that they're a little overweight, and think things like, "I hate the way I look," or "I look disgusting." When you say something like that about yourself, that means there's too much anxiety and sadness taking up space in your mind.

But when you sit in silence and really listen to your body, you can't hide from these truths anymore. And more important, instead of addressing them with a sad and stressed mind, you'll be looking at yourself clearly. Instead of saying, "I hate how I look," you'll just say, "Hmmm. I'm getting a bit thick in the middle. Time to watch what I eat." And then, most important, you'll actually *do it*. Because when you meditate, you can change on a dime. When you let go of anxiety, you won't want to ease into a better you. You'll want to go there right away. Yes, the more you come to know your true self, the more you want to make that self better.

PURE CONSCIOUSNESS

After a few minutes of taking inventory of both your thoughts and body, you will begin to enter what I call the stage of "pure consciousness." This is a stage where your thoughts subside and through your mantra you are able to access the limitless pool of stillness inside of you.

My teacher Bob Roth describes the state of pure consciousness this way: Think of your mind as being like the ocean. On the surface of the ocean it's choppy and there are a lot of waves. That's your distracted mind.

But at the bottom of the ocean, it's still. That's your mind in a state of pure consciousness.

Why is it so important to spend time down there? Because as my friend David Lynch puts it, "Ideas are like fish. If you want to catch little fish, you can stay in the shallow water. But if you want to catch the big fish, you've got to go deeper. Down deep, the fish are more powerful and more pure. They're huge and abstract. And they're beautiful."

Not only is this the stage when you're going to catch the "big fish" in your mind, but it's also the stage that promotes the physical healing that comes through meditation.

It's in deep consciousness that the strain and stress that your thoughts have been placing on your nervous system will fade away. As you become more restful, the different parts of your brain will finally begin to reconnect, the stress on your amygdala will be fully reduced.

FALLING ASLEEP

Some people find that they occasionally fall asleep during their meditation. If you find this happening to you, don't get frustrated or worried. If you're tired, especially if you haven't been getting enough sleep, then it's not unusual for your body to look for that rest during your meditation.

So just like everything else you experience in meditation, don't fight the urge to sleep. Instead, if you find yourself getting sleepy, allow yourself to drift away for a bit. And when you do wake back up, gently return to your mantra.

As long as you're consistent with your practice, you'll find that after a while you won't get so tired anymore when you meditate.

And as that stress begins to go down, your blood pressure is going to go down too. And reducing high blood pressure and calming your nervous system are arguably the most beneficial physical aspects of meditation.

WHEN IT'S "OVER"

Okay, so you've been sitting in meditation, first engaging your thoughts and then slowly sinking into a state of pure consciousness. Your eyes are closed and your mantra has led you down deep into the ocean of stillness inside of you. Maybe you even caught a big fish!

So how do you know that your twenty minutes are up?

The easiest way is before you start to meditate, simply take your smartphone and set the timer for twenty minutes—but please set it on a soft or gentle alarm! This is because sounds can appear much louder when you're meditating. Like I said, sometimes when I'm meditating and I clear my throat or even just swallow, it sounds like a bomb just went off! Little sounds that you wouldn't even notice during the course of your normal day might sound like they are coming through movie theater speakers when you meditate.

The issue is when your phone's buzzer goes off, it can not only be very jarring, but it can also negatively affect how much you take away from your session.

This is because when your session is over, you want to eaaase your way back into the world. If you jump up startled when your buzzer goes off and open your eyes right away, you're going to lose a lot of the benefits of the restfulness you just experienced.

It's similar to how you can't just jump in your car and drive off on a frigid day. Instead, you have to take a minute and let it warm up so it can adjust to the conditions. Your mind is the same way after meditation. When that timer goes off, you shouldn't just open your eyes, pick up your phone, and start responding to e-mails you missed while you were meditating. Instead, give your mind a minute or so to adjust to coming out of that ocean of stillness and back into the world.

I remember a scene in *Seinfeld* where Jerry was telling Elaine to let his car warm up for a minutes before she drove it, and George chimed in, "That's a tough minute. It's like waiting in the shower for

It might seem like obvious advice, but if you decide to use the timer on your phone, make sure all its other notification settings—like e-mail, phone calls, and texts—are turned off. Just like you don't want your phone ringing during the middle of a movie or a lecture, you don't want to find out you got a new text or e-mail during your meditation.

If this begins to be a problem for you, but you still feel like you need a timer, just turn your phone completely off and use an old-fashioned egg timer (preferably one that doesn't tick though) or stopwatch.

the conditioner to work." Well, letting yourself "warm up" after meditating can be a tough minute too at first, but don't give in to any temptation you feel to rush back into the world. You don't have to keep repeating your mantra, but at least keep your eyes closed. Just listen to yourself breathe and try to soak up all the peacefulness you just experienced, so that you can carry it with you as you reenter the world.

One of the primary reasons I recommend using a timer for beginners especially is because at first it's easy for them to be distracted by worrying about whether they've been meditating "long enough."

If you're struggling with discomfort, distractions, or even both, time might feel like it's moving slowly. To the point where you might begin to ask yourself, "Hasn't it been twenty minutes yet? I feel like

KEEP GOING!

I often get asked, "Is it okay if I meditate longer than twenty minutes?" And the answer is, "Of course!" If that timer goes off, but you're enjoying the bliss so much that you don't want to stop, then don't. Twenty minutes is only a recommended minimum time. If you want to go for another ten or fifteen minutes, just press "alarm off" and keep going!

I've been doing this for a long time." And instead of focusing on your mantra, you're constantly opening your eyes and checking the clock. Which is going to prevent you from truly slipping into a state of pure consciousness.

But once you set that timer to twenty minutes and press "start," you won't have the excuse of checking the clock to fall back on. Even if it feels like you've been going for more than twenty minutes, you'll know that if you haven't heard the buzzer, then you just need to consider that distraction for a moment and let it go.

One of the major benefits of meditation is reducing stress, so to stress over whether you've been meditating "long enough" would be extremely counterproductive.

When that timer does go off, remember that no matter how many minutes you've rested in stillness, you're going to be better off for it, not only in that day, but for the rest of your life. Take a few moments to acknowledge what you've accomplished and be grateful for it.

Notice how relaxed and contented you feel and allow yourself to marinate in that sensation for several more moments. You don't have to count to sixty or set your timer for an extra minute. Just soak in all that peacefulness until you feel ready to return to the world.

Then open your eyes.

HOW YOU'LL FEEL

When you finally do open your eyes and "reenter" the world, you'll feel a difference immediately. The feeling isn't the same every time, since every meditation is different. But you'll *always* feel better than you did before you started meditating.

If you went to bed and woke up with a stuffy nose, chances are it'll be cleared up a few minutes into your session. If you woke up with a headache, that'll probably be gone too. Certainly if you woke up feeling stressed about the day ahead of you, after twenty minutes those worries won't be weighing on you as heavily anymore. Again, this is because meditation is finally giving your nervous system a chance to calm down. Even when you're asleep, your nervous system is still often working overtime. So when it finally gets a chance to rest during meditation, you'll be amazed at how quickly your body can heal itself.

Clearing up stuffy noses and getting rid of headaches are just some of what I call the "normal" post-meditation effects. On other days, when you finally do open your eyes, the room might appear brighter and prettier than it did before. Colors will seem more vivid and alive. You'll notice the birds chirping outside and appreciate their beautiful melodies. You might even feel a little silly. Lots of mornings, I certainly start giggling because my appreciation of life is so much more vibrant. It sounds like a funny thing for a hip-hop guy to say, but a lot of times I even experience tears of joy.

When you begin to feel more alive and energized day in and day out, you'll be entering a state of what I call walking meditation. Where you are *extending* that sense of stillness *out* of your meditation and *into* your day. It might only last an hour or two before it begins to fade, but it's still an amazing experience for even that short amount of time. When you get a glimpse of how you could be living your entire life, it's going to inspire you to become even more dedicated to your practice.

Again, that sensation doesn't happen after just one or two practices. To live in a state of walking meditation, you must make the practice a permanent part of your lifestyle. But for now, just have faith that the more you practice, the more regularly that state will appear. Until eventually you will be able to make the state of connectedness your "normal" state. The famous guru Maharishi Mahesh Yogi—who taught the Beatles to meditate and started the Transcendental Meditation movement—once described the process this way to *Science of Mind* magazine:

> The situation is as though we were to take a white cloth and dip it in yellow dye. We bring the cloth out and put it in the sun and the yellow fades away. Then we put it back again and again into the color and back again and again into the sun.

In the dye it keeps on becoming yellow and yellow and yellow, then fading, fading, fading in the sun. But over time the color becomes permanent. That happens to the mind through regular practice. That unbounded awareness, that pure consciousness, the field of all the laws of nature, becomes ingrained in all activities of the mind.

Never forget that we all have the ability to turn our white cloths yellow over time. It might be a grind at first, but if you are patient with the process, eventually the change in you will become permanent. In time the noise of the world is going to fade out and you'll be able to hear your higher self all the time. Instead of a fleeting, momentary experience, that unbounded awareness will become ingrained in your mind. This is why it's so important to practice meditation *every day*. Gaining lasting happiness can only come through sustained, consistent effort. You're not going to get muscles from one push-up. Just as you're not going to lose twenty pounds just by skipping one meal. Or let go of the burdens of the world after sitting in silence for twenty minutes just one time. In order to achieve lasting happiness in this lifetime, you must make a real commitment to this process.

PATIENCE IS THE KEY

The final piece of advice I want to give you on your practice is very simple:

Be patient!

Again, every single one of us is capable of experiencing the happiness that comes from stillness. You just have to be patient and stick with the practice. As Deepak has always told me, "Russell, the number one tool every meditator must have is patience."

In fact, a funny thing happened when I first started writing this book. I was sitting on an airplane working on one of the chapters when I felt someone settle into the seat across from me. I was so focused on what I was writing that I didn't look up, but after a few moments I felt a tap on my arm. When I looked up, who was sitting there but Deepak!

I told him what I was working on and he smiled and said, "Russell, please tell your readers that while it takes time for every fruit to ripen, eventually they will all fall from the tree."

After he said that, I was the one who had to smile, because it was such a beautiful way to express the importance of sticking with this practice. Just like fruit, people take time to ripen.

Sometimes I have to remind myself of this truth. Believe me, there are mornings when I roll over to meditate and it feels like my mind is fighting me every step of the way.

When I'm having one of those mornings, I'll *gently* remind my mind who is the boss. I'll think, "Brotha, you can make all the noise you want. But you're still going to be sitting here with me for these twenty minutes." And when my mind hears that, when it realizes that it's not going to trick me into getting up and giving up, then it usually settles down pretty quickly.

Take your time and let your mind settle. You might want it to happen right away, but wanting things to happen on your own terms is probably what has you stressed out in the first place. Take your time and remember that what I'm promoting isn't a race toward being present. Instead, I'm just helping you start the journey to where you are supposed to be. And then have faith that if you stay on this path I've laid out before you, in short time you are going to find the incredible jewels that are waiting for you within your own mind.

FURTHER READING

As I mentioned, please don't be rigid or inflexible in your approach to meditation. If this book is able, as I know it can, to help you transform your life, then it will likely be all you need on the subject. But if after reading this you are motivated to learn more about meditation, by all means I encourage you to do so.

A great place to visit is TM.org, which is where you can learn even more about that practice and how to meet with an instructor from the organization. TM does charge a fee for new students, but they're also always flexible in taking people's situations into account. As Bob Roth put it to me, they've never once turned down someone who wanted to learn TM because they couldn't afford it.

Also be sure to check out DavidLynchFoundation.org, where you can find out more about all the wonderful outreach that organization does, including work with young people, veterans, and American Indians.

In terms of books, please make it a point to read two ancient texts: the Yoga Sūtras of Patañjali and the Bhagavad Gita. They might come off a little dense initially, but I promise you that they contain incredible insights into the type of bliss meditation will be taking you toward. The same is true for Yogananda's *Autobiography of a Yogi*. It's one of the most important books ever written on meditation and spirituality. It's especially powerful for those looking to reconcile the yogic and Christian traditions.

I also strongly recommend two books by Eckhart Tolle, *The Power of Now* and *A New Earth*. They describe presence in a much simpler, and more eloquent, way than I ever could. These books were a great eye-opener to me and helped me understand how being present is our only goal on earth.

Another great book to help you understand the mind-body connection is my friend Deepak Chopra's *The Seven Spiritual Laws of Success*.

And finally, I'd also welcome you to check out two of my own books, *Do You!* and *Super Rich*. They both explain how one can use the power inside of oneself to access true happiness and success.

ACKNOWLEDGMENTS

Many people have helped guide me down the path to stillness, but I'd like to thank two great inspirations in particular: Deepak Chopra and my partner in crime, Bob Roth, aka the Monk.